LOGIC, ANYONE?

165 BRAIN-STRETCHING LOGIC PROBLEMS   BEVERLY POST AND SANDRA EADS

Fearon Teacher Aids • Carthage, Illinois

Editor: Buff Bradley
Production editor: Gustavo Medina
Managing designer: Susan True
Designer: Joe di Chiarro
Illustrator: Duane Bibby
Cover designer: Joe di Chiarro

Acknowledgments

Dr. William S. Puett, Professor of Philosophy at California
State University, Dominguez Hills. His knowledge and
expertise aided us in insuring the authenticity and accuracy
of the logical concepts and procedures in the book.

Robert S. Hopkins, M.A. We appreciate his encouragement
and wise advice.

To our patient families. Thank you.

ISBN 0-8224-4326-0

Printed in the United States of America
1.14

CONTENTS

INTRODUCTION

The ability to think clearly and reason logically is a primary goal of education, and can be taught to children in a way that is interesting and fun. In an information-saturated era, when this morning's facts are this afternoon's artifacts, a person must be able to think clearly, analyze information, and reason logically.

SIX TYPES OF LOGIC PROBLEMS

Logic, Anyone? presents six types of logic problems—analogies, matrix logic, table logic, circle logic, syllogisms, and Venn Diagrams. Step-by-step work pages introduce each type of problem, then lead students through the process of understanding and solving the problems that follow. A reminder page follows each set of work pages, detailing key points to remember when working the problems. The problems themselves are arranged in order of increasing difficulty: The last problems in each section are significantly harder than the first. By doing the easier problems first, students prepare themselves to tackle the more demanding ones at the end.

Each section concludes with three pages that help students make up their own logic problems to try on their friends. Students will find that constructing their own logic problems can be at least as demanding as solving problems made by others, and that it further builds the thinking skills used to solve logic problems.

HOW TO USE THIS BOOK

Much of the material in *Logic, Anyone?* originally was developed for the gifted, but it also has been used successfully with students, aged eight through fourteen, who are not necessarily identified as gifted.

In the classroom, the logic problems can be used in any of three ways: (1) as independent activities at learning centers; (2) as extra or supplementary work for advanced students and/or those who finish assigned work early; or (3) as a kind of mini-course in thinking skills, in "concentrated" form, for the entire class.

The work pages and problem pages in *Logic, Anyone?* are designed to be self-explanatory—most students should be able to do them without help from the teacher. If the whole class is working on the problems at once, however, it might be a good idea for the teacher to introduce the material, perhaps leading the group through the work pages and even through the solution of the first problem or two. After that, students can work on their own. Some students will be eager to race through all the problems in a section; others will want to take more time. The pace is up to the teacher, who is responsible for duplicating and distributing the problems. For the most part, it's probably a good idea to take a few days with each section, encouraging students to make up problems to challenge one another, so that the material can be reinforced.

At the back of the book is an Answer Key, for use in correcting problems. The teacher may choose from among three alternatives regarding correction of problems: (1) collecting the students' completed problems and correcting them; (2) duplicating the Answer Key pages and laminating them so that students can correct their own work; or (3) reading the answers aloud to the entire group when all students are finished. This last alternative allows for further discussion and clarification, which will be particularly helpful when checking answers to the Venn Diagrams. In fact, the answers to the Venn Diagram problems include a brief discussion of the rationale for each answer.

PROBLEMS THAT ARE FUN TO WORK

Although the activities in *Logic, Anyone?* are called logic *problems,* they are more like puzzles, but with one important difference—there are no tricks. Like good puzzles, these logic activities are fun and stretch the brain. In introducing these problems to students, the teacher may want to emphasize their puzzlelike qualities to heighten students' motivation. While students are enjoying themselves working these puzzles/games/problems, they will also be working toward a very serious goal—developing the ability to think, organize, analyze, and arrive at logical conclusions.

ANALOGIES

An analogy is a logical way of making a comparison. Here is an example of an analogy:

Hot is to *cold* as *near* is to *far.*

An analogy compares relationships between two different sets. In the example, the two sets are *hot/cold* and *near/far.* Each two items in a set have a special relationship. The subjects of the sets can be different (*hot* and *cold* are about temperature; *near* and *far* are about distance). But the items in one set must be related to each other in the same way as the items in the other set.

Here's how that works. Start with one set—*hot* and *cold.* What is the relationship between these two? Underline the correct answer.

They: **1)** mean the same thing; **2)** mean almost the same thing;
    3) are opposites

ANSWER: Of course, they are opposites.

Now here's the other set—*near* and *far.* What is the relationship between these two? Underline the correct answer.

They: **1)** mean the same thing; **2)** mean almost the same thing;
    3) are opposites

ANSWER: Again, they are opposites.

What is the relationship between *hot* and *cold*? _____

What is the relationship between *near* and *far*? _____

ANSWER: Yes, opposites.

Since the relationships are the same, we can say, "Hot is to cold as near is to far," and we have made an analogy.

Let's try another analogy, using *leaf* and *tree* in one set and *petal* and *flower* in the other set.

What is the relationship between *leaf* and *tree*? Underline the correct answer:

They are: **1)** not a part of a whole; **2)** the same; **3)** a part of a whole

ANSWER: They are a part of a whole.

What is the relationship between *petal* and *flower*? Underline the correct answer.

They are: **1)** not a part of a whole; **2)** the same; **3)** a part of a whole

ANSWER: They are a part of a whole.

Are the relationships of the two sets the same? Can we say that leaf is to tree as petal is to flower? _____

ANSWER: Yes.

When the relationship in the first set is the same as the relationship in the second set, that is an analogy.

Now you must select the final word to correctly complete the following analogy:

Feathers are to *bird* as *fur* is to _____ .

(dog, fish, snake, skin)

Look for the relationship between the first two. Then find the word that makes the same relationship between the second two. The answer is *dog*. Feathers cover birds and fur covers dogs.

One more thing before you go on: Notice the order of the words in both sets. Be sure the relationships in the word sets, or pairs, are in the same order.

Feathers are to *bird* as *dog* is to *fur* is not in the correct order. This makes the relationships not the same.

Write the analogy correctly.

_____

ANSWER: Feathers are to bird as fur is to dog.

Now that you understand analogies, you can do analogy problems on your own. First read the reminders on the Analogies Reminder Page. Then do the problems. Refer to the Analogies Reminder Page if you have trouble completing any of the analogies.

ANALOGIES REMINDER PAGE

- An analogy is a comparison of relationships between two different sets.

- The subjects of the sets are different, but the relationships are the same.

- Look for the relationship in the first set. Quickly survey the second set of choices for a similar relationship. Some relationships are:

    Part of a whole
    Opposites
    The same
    Time sequence (before or after, for example)

- Compare the two sets to see that the relationship in each set is the same.

- The words in both sets must be in the same order. For example, if the first set is *a part to whole,* the second set must be *a part to whole,* **not** *whole to a part.*

- An analogy has a special form. It is always written in the same way:

_____ is to _____ as _____ is to _____.

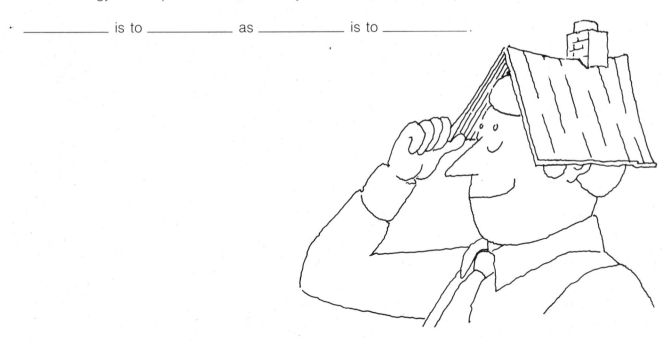

1. Tall is to short as night is to _____ .
   day, right, long, dark

2. Happy is to glad as angry is to _____ .
   smile, scared, mad, curious

3. Fish is to water as bird is to _____ .
   air, feather, sea, wing

4. Bulb is to light as furnace is to _____ .
   cold, summer, fire, heat

5. Hand is to glove as head is to _____ .
   foot, face, hat, neck

6. Few is to many as less is to _____ .
   several, more, big, fewer

7. Height is to tall as width is to _____ .
   wide, fat, round, thin

8. Ship is to water as airplane is to _____ .
   waves, air, flight, cloud

9. House is to roof as head is to _____ .
   top, tile, hair, neck

10. Seldom is to often as few is to _____ .
    several, many, rarely, more

11. Wall is to brick as skeleton is to _____ .
   skull, legs, bone, flesh

12. Hand is to clock as needle is to _____ .
   watch, compass, number, face

13. Key is to lock as door is to _____ .
   wall, knob, floor, hinge

14. Bulb is to lamp as engine is to _____ .
   light, wheel, car, tree

15. Paint is to wall as skin is to _____ .
   eyes, body, hair, hands

16. Cat is to mouse as police officer is to _____ .
   gun, bandit, patrolman, constable

17. Sail is to boat as engine is to _____ .
   battery, go, car, drive

18. Seed is to fruit as pilot is to _____ .
   engine, radio, cockpit, wing

19. Mom is to dad as sister is to _____ .
   boy, male, child, brother

20. Cupboard is to dishes as house is to _____ .
   roof, windows, door, people

21. Warm is to boiling as cold is to _____.
    frost, colder, ice, freezing

22. Sun is to day as moon is to _____.
    stars, night, bright, space

23. Robin is to bird as yellow is to _____.
    red, sunlight, color, light

24. Tadpole is to frog as caterpillar is to _____.
    egg, butterfly, fly, skin

25. Tie is to shirt as butter is to _____.
    spread, bread, buttermilk, cream

26. Past is to horse as present is to _____.
    sled, bicycle, cart, car

27. Poster is to wall as stamp is to _____.
    envelope, note, mail, post office

28. Picture is to frame as door is to _____.
    house, molding, window, floor

29. Horse is to hay as rabbit is to _____.
    apple, tomato, carrot, spinach

30. Dog is to leash as balloon is to _____.
    string, air, clown, party

31. Cola is to drink as bread is to _____.
  jam, sandwich, lunch, eat

32. Eye is to see as nose is to _____.
  face, sneeze, smell, sunburn

33. Fish is to scales as crab is to _____.
  sand, shell, ocean, rocks

34. Film is to camera as ink is to _____.
  pen, write, letter, blot

35. Pig is to sty as horse is to _____.
  barn, hay, saddle, hoof

36. Ping pong is to paddle as croquet is to _____.
  wicket, mallet, ball, hat

37. Baseball is to mitt as golf is to _____.
  net, tee, racket, bat

38. Page is to book as bone is to _____.
  joint, skin, body, leg

39. Camel is to animal as apple is to _____.
  orange, fruit, delicious, red

40. Dime is to money as German is to _____.
  speak, silent, talk, language

41. Sacramento is to California as Salem is to _____.
    Washington, Utah, Oregon, Colorado

42. Car is to gas as human being is to _____.
    eat, digest, food, fuel

43. Rim is to glass as peak is to _____.
    plane, mountain, plateau, crevice

44. Hour is to clock as mile is to _____.
    altimeter, odometer, thermometer, barometer

45. Predator is to prey as hawk is to _____.
    fly, frog, hare, beak

46. Blood is to vein as water is to _____.
    lake, aqueduct, reservoir, pump

47. Hear is to deaf as likeness is to _____.
    difference, picture, image, sameness

48. Enormous is to huge as look is to _____.
    read, view, eyes, senses

49. Monday is to Tuesday as Friday is to _____.
    Thursday, Sunday, Saturday, Wednesday

50. Melody is to tune as speech is to _____.
    silence, talk, automatic, language

MAKE YOUR OWN ANALOGIES

Begin by adding the second set, or pair of words, to the following analogies. Remember: The relationships must be the same, but the subjects will be different.

1. Sad is to happy as _____ is to _____ .

2. Weak is to strong as _____ is to _____ .

3. Dark is to light as _____ is to _____ .

4. Baking is to bread as _____ is to _____ .

5. Actor is to movie as _____ is to _____ .

Now test your ability to see a relationship between words. For more practice, fill in the following blanks.

1. Funny is to _____ as _____ is to _____ .

2. Down is to _____ as _____ is to _____ .

3. Tired is to _____ as _____ is to _____ .

4. Run is to _____ as _____ is to _____ .

5. Child is to _____ as _____ is to _____ .

MAKE YOUR OWN ANALOGIES

Try writing some analogies on your own. Begin by thinking of a subject. Next, think of something that relates to it or is a part of it. The next step is the most difficult, but this is where the fun comes in—think up a subject that's entirely different but that can relate in the same way as your first set related.

Be sure that you write your problem in the correct way. Use this form when you are writing analogies. See how many analogies you can create.

1. _____ is to _____ as _____ is to _____ .

2. _____ is to _____ as _____ is to _____ .

3. _____ is to _____ as _____ is to _____ .

4. _____ is to _____ as _____ is to _____ .

5. _____ is to _____ as _____ is to _____ .

6. _____ is to _____ as _____ is to _____ .

7. _____ is to _____ as _____ is to _____ .

8. _____ is to _____ as _____ is to _____ .

9. _____ is to _____ as _____ is to _____ .

10. _____ is to _____ as _____ is to _____ .

When you're finished, ask someone—a teacher, a friend, a parent—to read your analogies and see if they're all correct.

MAKE YOUR OWN ANALOGIES

Use the form below to create analogies for your friends to solve. Begin your problem in the same way as before: Fill in the first three blanks (the first set, and half of the second set) but *don't* fill in the fourth blank. In the numbered spaces under each analogy, write four words. One of these should be the correct answer to your problem. Don't make the choices too easy!

1. _____ is to _____ as _____ is to _____.

(1. _____ 2. _____ 3. _____ 4. _____)

2. _____ is to _____ as _____ is to _____.

(1. _____ 2. _____ 3. _____ 4. _____)

3. _____ is to _____ as _____ is to _____.

(1. _____ 2. _____ 3. _____ 4. _____)

4. _____ is to _____ as _____ is to _____.

(1. _____ 2. _____ 3. _____ 4. _____)

5. _____ is to _____ as _____ is to _____.

(1. _____ 2. _____ 3. _____ 4. _____)

6. _____ is to _____ as _____ is to _____.

(1. _____ 2. _____ 3. _____ 4. _____)

MATRIX LOGIC

To do matrix logic problems, start by gathering information from clues. These clues can be tricky. One clue may give you only a little information by itself, but it may give a lot more information when you fit it together with another clue. Here's how it works:

CANDY, CANDY, CANDY

Find out what kind of candy Tina, Kathryn, and Jacky like. Each child likes only one kind, and no two children like the same kind.

1. Tina hates chocolate bars.

2. Kathryn eats taffy.

(Since each child likes only one kind of candy, you know that

Kathryn doesn't like _____ .

ANSWER: Chocolate bars.

And since Kathryn likes taffy, and no two children like the same kind

of candy, you now know that Tina also doesn't like _____ .)

ANSWER: Taffy.

3. Jacky hates lollipops.

(Now you know what all three candies are:

_____ , _____ , and _____ .

ANSWER: Chocolate bars, taffy, lollipops.

Since each child likes only one kind of candy, and Tina doesn't

like chocolate bars or taffy, she must like _____ .

ANSWER: Lollipops.

Since Tina likes _____ , and Kathryn likes _____ ,

ANSWER: Tina likes lollipops, Kathryn likes taffy.

there's only one kind of candy that Jacky could like, and it's

_____ .)

ANSWER: Chocolate bars.

To keep track of all the information in this kind of problem, record it on a chart called a *matrix*. Using the matrix below, write down the three children's names in the boxes on the side, and the three kinds of candy in the boxes on the top.

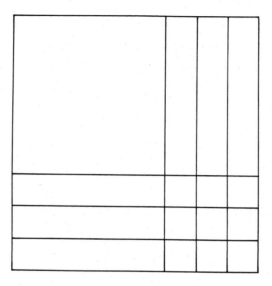

Now use the matrix to record the information you get from each of the clues.

1. Tina hates chocolate bars.

(Mark a big *X* in the box where *Tina* and *chocolate bars* meet.)

2. Kathryn eats taffy.

(Write *Yes* where *Kathryn* and *taffy* meet. Then mark *X* in the other two boxes next to Kathryn's name, since she only likes one kind of candy. Finally, mark *X* where *Tina* and *taffy* meet, and where *Jacky* and *taffy* meet—since each child likes only one candy, and Kathryn likes taffy, this means that Tina and Jacky don't like taffy.)

3. Jacky hates lollipops.

(Mark *X* in the box where *Jacky* and *lollipops* meet. Now you can see that there's only one space left next to Tina's name—*lollipops*. Mark that box *Yes*. And there's only one space left next to Jacky's name—*chocolate bars*. Mark that box *Yes*.)

Here's what your completed matrix should look like:

	chocolate bars	taffy	lollipops
Tina	X	X	yes
Kathryn	X	yes	X
Jacky	yes	X	X

You can chart all matrix problems the way you just charted the children-and-candy problem. A more complicated problem will have more boxes. If you have three people's names, their food choices, and their drink choices, you can use a matrix like the one below.

Fill in the following information:

1. Use the children's names: Pat, James, and Laura.
2. The foods are: pizza, fish, and hot dogs.
3. The drinks are: lemonade, cola, and milk.

The next kind of matrix is used for even more complex problems. Using the four clues that follow, try filling in as much of the matrix as you can. **You cannot solve the entire problem because you do not have all the clues.** But for practice, fill in what you can.

HOUSES, BOYS, AND PETS

Billy Brown, Willie White, Bobby Blue, and George Green all live on the same street. All four of their houses are painted colors that do not match their last names. Also, each boy has a pet, and its name does not begin with the same letter as its owner's name. On top of that, you must find out the location of each house; is it first, second, third, or fourth on the block? (You will need three categories at the top of your matrix.)

1. George Green owns the bear.
2. Willie White owns the bull.
3. Neither the bear nor the bull lives next to the first house.
4. The white house is the last one on the street.

	House Color				Location				Pet			
	Brown	White	Green	Blue	First	Second	Third	Fourth	Worm	Bear	Gorilla	Bull
Billy Brown												
Willie White												
George Green												
Bobby Blue												

It is easy to chart clues 1 and 2. The third clue is a little tricky; the bear and the bull couldn't live in the second house.

The fourth clue only gives you partial information, not enough to mark your matrix. In a case like this, you must write a note above the appropriate box to help you later in solving the problem. (See the matrix for this problem on page 109 of the Answer Key.)

MATRIX LOGIC REMINDER PAGE

- First read all the clues and write all the names and categories in the matrix.

- Find all clues that give a definite yes or no. (For example: Kathryn eats taffy. Tina hates chocolate.) Mark boxes with X or Yes. Remember that whenever you mark a box Yes, you can then put Xs in all the other boxes in the row next to it and all the boxes in the row above and below it.

- Find all clues that give some information, but not enough to tell you how to mark boxes. Using those clues, make notes above boxes that you can use when you go back over all the clues.

- Go over each clue again carefully and relate it to other clues. Find two or more clues that fit together to give enough information to mark boxes Yes or X (No).

1. FLOWERS

Karen, Derek, Fay, Tanya, and Scott each have a special favorite flower. No two of them have the same favorite. Which child goes with which flower?

1. Karen's favorite is not the tulip.
2. Derek hates tulips and roses.
3. Someone really likes daisies.
4. Fay likes violets.
5. Tanya is allergic to carnations.
6. Scott likes the flower to which Tanya is allergic.

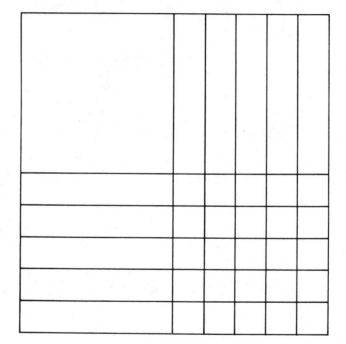

2. THE ARTISTS

Mark, Meg, Melissa, and Marcie are all artists. One child uses only felt pens, one child uses only black pencils, one child uses only water colors, and one child uses only crayons. Find out what each child uses.

1. Melissa loves to use bright colors but doesn't enjoy felt pens.
2. Marcie and Melissa never have paint on their hands, but their friend does.
3. Mark takes excellent care of his brushes.
4. Meg thinks black pencils are boring.

3. CLEANING DAY

Mrs. Bailey tells each of her five children that they must clean one room each week. The rooms that need to be cleaned are the living room, den, kitchen, bathroom, and one bedroom. Which room does each child clean?

1. Darla really dislikes cleaning sinks.
2. Connie hates making beds.
3. Jay and Troy always turn the cushions on the couches when they clean.
4. The den is right next to the kitchen; Troy and Phil enjoy talking to each other as they work.
5. There are no couches in the kitchen, bathroom, or bedroom.

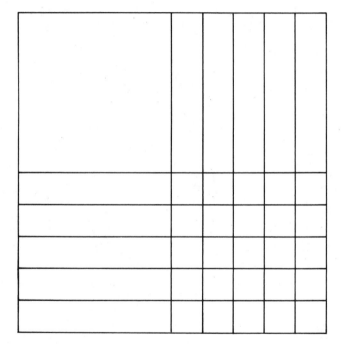

4. FAMILY VACATION

The Grand family wants to choose the perfect place for a vacation, but they have some difficulty making the final decision. Finally, they decide on Lake Z because it is the best place to do their favorite activity. Which activity do they enjoy most: fishing, hiking, camping, or swimming? Which activities do the other lakes offer?

1. Lake Z and Lake F have no camping facilities.
2. Lake S does not allow swimming.
3. Lake R has dried up.
4. There are no fish in Lake F or Lake Z.
5. Lake F is known for excellent hiking.

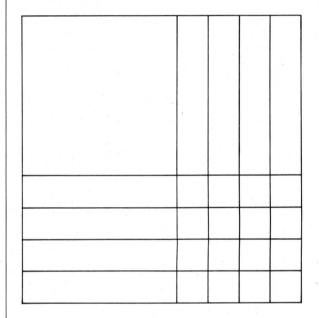

5. PIANO LESSONS

Three children in one family are taking piano lessons. The family has a schedule that gives each child an hour to practice. The practice hours are 3:00, 5:00, and 9:00. Find out when each child practices.

1. Betty practices at either 5:00 or at 9:00.
2. Bob doesn't practice at 5:00.
3. Brenda doesn't practice at 9:00.
4. Betty doesn't practice at 3:00.
5. Bob practices two hours before Brenda.

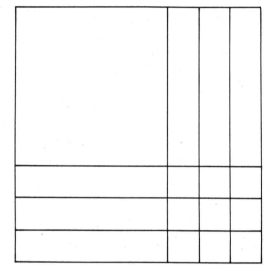

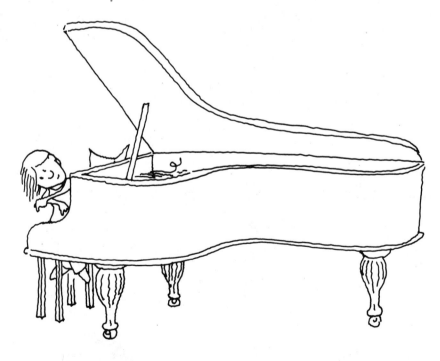

6. WHO LIVES WHERE?

Three children live in different-colored houses on three different streets.
Find out the name of the street and the color of each child's house.

1. Cathy's house is orange.
2. Cathy's best friend lives in a red house.
3. Brian's address is 2910 Lake Street.
4. Cathy's best friend is Joann.
5. Cathy's best friend lives on Anza Avenue.
6. Brian's house is brown with steps in front.
7. Someone lives on Maple.

7. FIND THE SPORT

Each of five children like to play one particular sport. No two like the same sport. The children are Joe, Donna, Denise, Kent, and Scott. The sports that they like to play are soccer, baseball, hockey, football, and kickball. Which sport does each play?

1. Joe doesn't like to play soccer.
2. Donna has never played football and neither has Joe.
3. Denise does not play kickball.
4. Joe doesn't like to play baseball.
5. Joe and Scott do not like to kick balls—it hurts their toes.
6. Scott is a great hitter and he gets a lot of practice in his favorite sport.
7. Denise has always liked soccer the best of all sports.

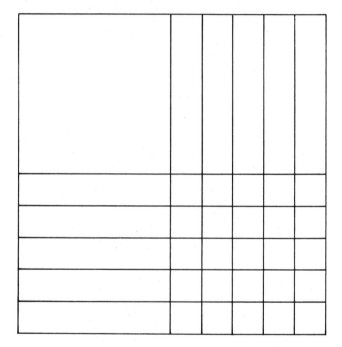

8. CAREERS

Don, Robert, and Laura have chosen careers as a teacher, a plumber, and a house painter. Find out the career and the correct age of each person.

1. Don would not like to be a teacher.
2. Robert is not 25 years old, but his friend is.
3. The plumber is not 30 years old.
4. Lee's friend is 22 years old.
5. Don is 30 years old and his friend, Robert, is the one who works with children.

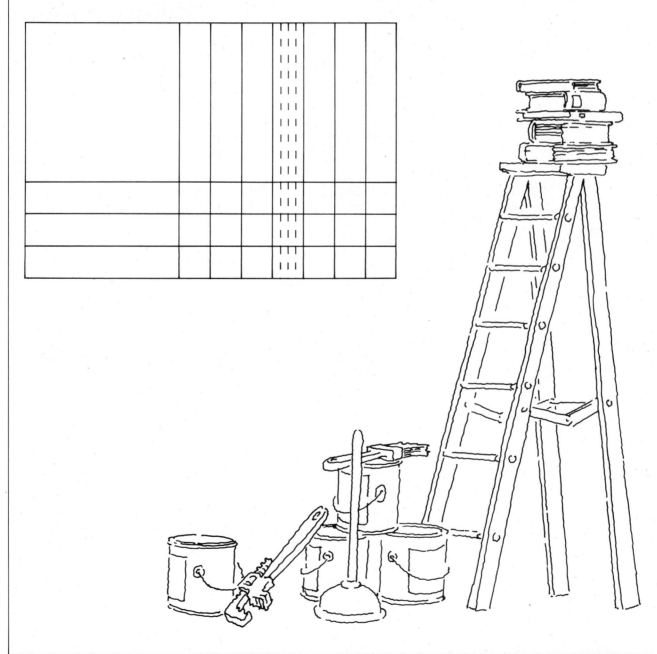

9. R.I.P.

Six good friends died within one week. Find out the order in which they died: first, second, third, fourth, fifth, sixth.

1. Jack died immediately after John.
2. Robert died right between Tony and Bill.
3. Fred died.
4. Robert died third.
5. John lived to see four funerals.
6. Tony died two days before Bill.

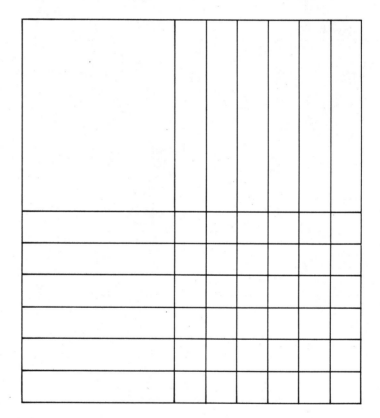

10. THIS IS NOT EASY

There are five children whom you would like to know better. Find out the ages of each child and the color of each child's house. You will need two categories at the top of your matrix. Filling in the matrix for this problem is tricky. You must read each of the clues very carefully to find out the colors and the ages to write in the boxes at the top.

1. Sean's house is red.
2. Julie is 9 years older than Sean.
3. Kim is 4; she is 2 years older than Sean.
4. Mary's house is the opposite color of Ted's house.
5. Sean's age rhymes with blue.
6. Julie's favorite color is blue; that is also the color of her house.
7. Julie and Kim are sisters.
8. Mary is 11 years older than Ted.
9. Ted is 4 years older than Sean.
10. Ted's house is painted black.

11. CIRCUS TIME

Four children go to see the circus. Each child has a favorite circus animal, and each one likes a certain circus food. Find out the children's names, their favorite animals, and the foods they like. Each child's choice is different.

1. Jimmy likes camels.
2. Amy hates popcorn.
3. Bob likes ice cream.
4. Tracy likes lions but hates tigers.
5. Bob likes zebras but hates cotton candy.
6. Amy hates snow cones.
7. Jimmy eats snow cones but hates lions.

12. BIRTHDAY PARTIES

One week, there is a birthday party every day. No two children are invited to the same party. Find out the day that each child attends a party. Start your matrix with Sunday and continue on to Saturday.

1. Lisa and Pat don't go to a party on Friday or Saturday.
2. Pat and Alice don't go on a Tuesday, but Sandy does.
3. Jennifer goes to a party on Wednesday.
4. Jim goes to a party the day after Jennifer.
5. Lisa goes the day before Pat.
6. Paul goes on a Saturday.

13. HOTEL ROOMS

Five families decide to hold family reunions at a large hotel. Each family occupies a suite on a different floor. On which floor is each family? It won't be easy to figure out which floor numbers to write down on your matrix. Read the clues carefully!

1. The Carley family is on the floor directly under the Wright family.
2. The Malloy family is on a floor below all the others.
3. There is one floor between the Brown and Malloy families.
4. The Brown children have to ride the elevator up 17 floors to visit the Snows.
5. The Wright children are not on the 16th floor, but their friends the Carleys are. These same friends are 10 floors above the Malloys.

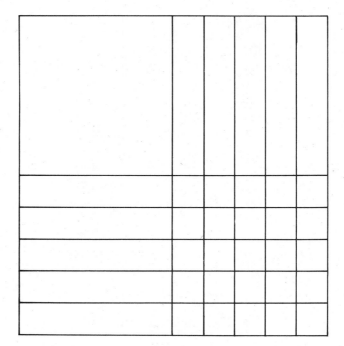

14. BEACH PARTY

Jeff, Ted, Steve, and Chris all go to the beach. When they get out of the water, they notice that someone has mixed up their shoes and towels. Figure out which items belong to each of the children.

1. Steve's towel and shoes are the same color.
2. The person with the blue sneakers has a red towel.
3. One of the children wears brown loafers.
4. Jeff has a green towel.
5. Jeff's shoes are the same color as Chris' towel.
6. If Chris' towel faded, it would be pink.
7. Ted has an infection in his toe and cannot wear open-toed shoes; he does not own the red sandals.
8. Steve would rather go barefoot than wear the green running shoes.
9. Steve either has the blue or the brown towel.

15. DETECTIVE DILEMMA

Sally has just finished a mystery book. Can you tell how it ended? Which detective found the real secret code book, what color was the book, and where was it located? Write notes next to some boxes to find out who solved the case.

1. Four detectives were looking for the code book. There was one real book and three fake books. Each book was a different color: blue, green, brown, and red.
2. Detective Zill found the brown book in a hidden wall panel.
3. The detective who found the blue book did not find it in the well.
4. The real book was not found in the cave or the safe; the fake books were found there.
5. Detective Thrill found a book in the well.
6. Detective Pill found the red book, but it was a phony.
7. Detective Mill did not find his book in the safe.
8. Detective Zill did not solve this case.

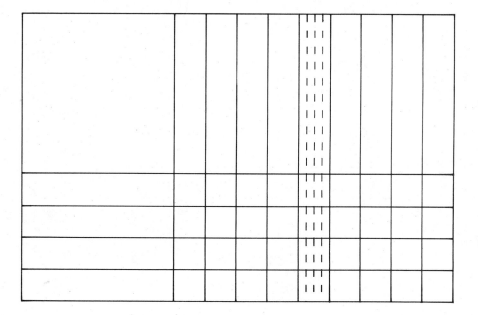

16. COLLECTIONS

Maureen, Joan, Robert, and Bryan each have two favorite hobbies, which include collections. The collections are seashells, stamps, baseball cards, coins, comic books, dolls, bugs, and rocks. No two children collect the same things. Find out the two collections that each child owns.

  (You will need to include all eight categories at the top of your matrix, and to allow each child *two* of the collections.) Be sure you have two Yeses for a child before you X the rest of the categories for the child.

1. Maureen always finds things for both of her collections outdoors.
2. Joan's friend enjoys collecting stamps.
3. One of Bryan's friends enjoys collecting coins.
4. The person who collects comics does not collect baseball cards.
5. One of Bryan's hobbies involves lots of reading.
6. Joan's family has a beach house; this is very helpful for one of her collections.
7. One of the girls collects dolls.

17. OCCUPATIONS

Four people have the following occupations: police officer, dress shop owner, teacher, and candy store owner. Match the person to his or her correct occupation. In this matrix, making notes above the boxes may help you solve the problem.

1. Kay and Jason met in a dress shop while one of them was buying a dress from the other.
2. Bill and Don met each other when one of them was buying candy from the other for his class.
3. Don and Kay met while one was giving the other a traffic ticket.
4. Don meets a friend at the Country Club every Tuesday at 10:00 a.m.

18. TALENT CONTEST

Ten people are finalists in a talent contest. For the final judging, they are lined up in order of the tallest to the shortest. Where does each person stand? Number the people from the tallest (#1) to the shortest (#10). You'll need to make lots of notes for this one!

1. Maria is standing next to Bill.
2. Ray is taller than Josh, who is standing next to Kim, who is shorter.
3. Bill is the tallest person.
4. Perin is taller than Kim, and they are both taller than Ruth.
5. No one is standing between Perin (the taller) and Abby.
6. No one is standing between Frances and Maria.
7. Abby is shorter than Abe, who is also shorter than Frances.
8. Abe is taller than Perin, who is taller than Ray; they are all taller than Kim.

19. PIZZA PARTY

Six friends go out for pizza. They soon find out that they can't share a large pizza because each person likes a different type. The friends end up ordering six individual pizzas: plain cheese; cheese and pepperoni; cheese, pepperoni, and sausage; cheese and anchovies; The Works; and cheese and bacon. Who orders what?

1. Kent likes only one item other than cheese, and that is not pepperoni.
2. Tom sits next to the person who orders cheese and bacon.
3. Fred hates any kind of fish.
4. The person who orders two items and cheese sits directly across from Betty.
5. Trina orders The Works.
6. Willie won't eat sausage or bacon.
7. Betty and Tom sit next to each other.
8. Fred and Tom both like pepperoni.

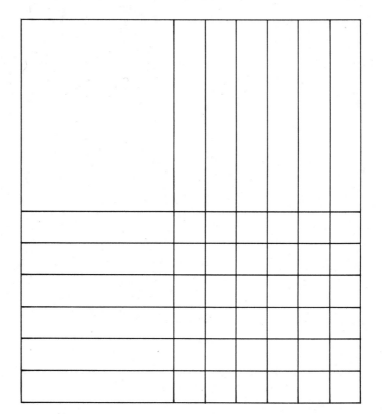

20. MORE HOUSES, BOYS, AND PETS

Billy Brown, Willie White, Bobby Blue, and George Green all live on the same street. Their houses are painted brown, white, blue, and green, but no boy lives in a house that matches his last name. Also, each boy has a pet, and its name does not begin with the same letter as its owner's name. On top of that, you must find out the location of each house—is it first, second, third, or fourth on the block?

1. George Green owns the bear.
2. Willie White owns the bull.
3. The white house is the last one on the street.
4. Neither the bear nor the bull live next to the first house.
5. Bobby Blue's house is not green.
6. The boy who owns the worm lives in the green house.
7. The gorilla lives in the first house, which is brown.

MAKE YOUR OWN MATRIX LOGIC PROBLEM

To start you off, try this:

1. Use the categories of *tennis, golf,* and *archery.*

2. Make up the names of three people.

3. Place the categories and names in the matrix (the names on the left, the categories at the top).

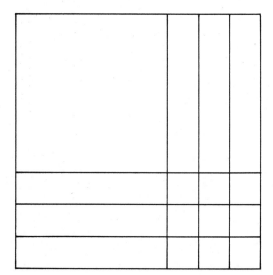

4. Fill in your desired answers.

5. Now write five clues that will lead to the solution of your problem.

A. _____

B. _____

C. _____

D. _____

E. _____

6. Now give the clues to a friend. Your friend must make a matrix and solve the problem.

MAKE YOUR OWN MATRIX LOGIC PROBLEM

This time, make up a problem using four kinds of food. Choose names for four people.

1. Place the categories and the names in the matrix below.

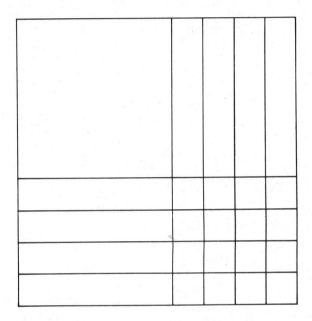

2. Select and fill in your answers to the matrix.

3. Now write clues that will lead to the solution of your problem.

A. _____

B. _____

C. _____

D. _____

E. _____

F. _____

4. Now give the clues to a friend. Your friend must make a matrix and solve the problem.

MAKE YOUR OWN MATRIX LOGIC PROBLEM

Try creating a problem using two different categories: colors and kinds of pets.

1. Select three different colors, three different kinds of pets, and three children's names.

2. Place the categories and names in the matrix.

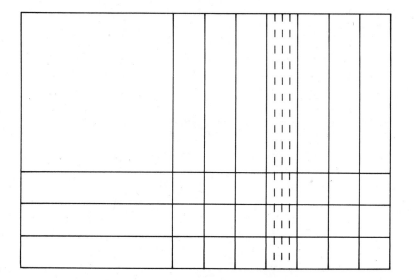

3. Decide on your answers and complete the matrix.

4. Make up clues that will lead to the solution of your problem.

   A. _____

   B. _____

   C. _____

   D. _____

   E. _____

5. Now give the clues to a friend. Your friend must make a matrix and solve the problem.

TABLE LOGIC

To do table logic problems, you must read the clues and figure out where each person sits at the table. The table looks like this:

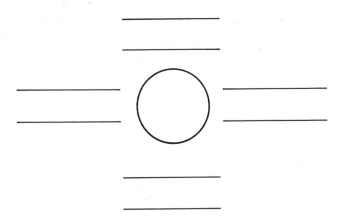

The blanks on each side are for the first and last names of the people sitting at the table. Write the first names on the top blank of each pair of lines; write the last names on the bottom blank.

Here is a table logic problem for you to try. Read the clues and figure out who sits where. Keep in mind that *partners always sit across from each other,* and that *people always sit facing the table.* Remember this when figuring out who sits to the right and left of whom.

THE CARD GAME

Four people—two women and two men—play this card game.

1. After the game, Ms. Lee vows never to be a partner with James

   again. (You know that Ms. Lee and James are _____, so

   they sit _____ each other.

   ANSWERS: Partners; across from.

   You can fill in their names—*Lee* on a bottom blank, *James* across
   from it on a top blank.)

2. Betty really doesn't care for Donna but has a wonderful time playing partners with Frank. (You know that the two women's first names are

_____ and _____ .

You also know that Betty and Frank are _____ and sit

_____ each other.

And you know that Ms. Lee's first name is not Betty because Ms. Lee's partner is James, and Betty's partner is Frank. Since there are only two women playing, Ms. Lee's first name must be

_____ .

Write her name on the blank above *Lee.*)

3. Frank sits to Donna's right. (You know where Frank sits. Write his name on the top blank to Donna's right. Since Frank and Betty are

partners, they sit _____ each other.

Also, there's only one place left. Write *Betty* on the top blank there.)

4. Mr. Davis sits next to Ms. Blake. (You know that Ms. Lee's first name

is _____ , so Betty's last name must be _____ .

Write her last name on the blank under *Betty.* You also know that

one of the men's last names is _____ .)

5. James and Frank are brothers. (If James and Frank are brothers, and one of the men's last name is Davis, the other's last name must

be _____ also.)

Finish filling in the blanks and check the table below to see how you did.

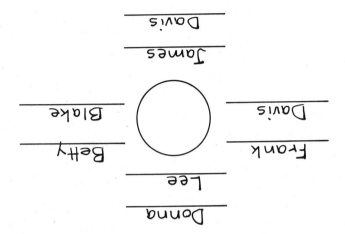

Here's another one for you to try. (*Mary* has been entered for you.)

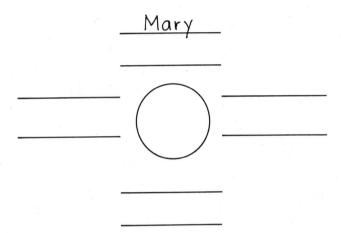

1. Four children are playing a new game called Dice-O. Mary and

Bobby are partners. (You know that Mary sits _____
Bobby.

ANSWER: Across from.

Write in *Bobby* on the top blank across from Mary.)

2. Every time Jane gets mad, she calls Jimmy by his whole
name—Jimmy Smith. (You know the other two children's first

names—_____ and _____.

ANSWERS: Jane; Jimmy.

You also know one player's last name—_____.

ANSWER: Smith.

You know that those two are partners and sit _____
each other.

But you don't yet know where they belong. Go on to the next clue.)

3. Bobby is left-handed and keeps bumping Jane's arm every time he throws the dice. (Since Bobby is left-handed, he must have

bumped the person on his _____ . That person is _____ .

If she is on Bobby's left, Bobby is on her _____ .

Write her name where it belongs. She and Jimmy are partners, so

Jimmy Smith goes _____ her.)

4. This is probably the first and last time that the sisters and brothers in that family have played Dice-O. (Now you know that all the children have the same last name, since they are sisters and brothers. Fill in the rest of the blanks. Check the table below to see how you did.)

TABLE LOGIC REMINDER PAGE

- In table logic problems, *partners* always sit *opposite* each other.

- People always sit *facing the table.* Remember that when you are figuring out who sits to the left and right of whom.

- Write each person's first name on the top line and the last name on the bottom line.

- Read each clue very carefully—it may have more than one hint.

- Enter sure facts only—no guessing.

- You may need to skip a clue and then go back to it later.

- The tables in the answer section may look a little different from yours. Don't let this worry you—just make sure that each person has the correct partner and the correct people on the right and left.

1. KID'S GAME

It is a rainy day. Four friends decide to play a card game. Where does each child sit? You need to know only their first names.

1. Paul, Mike, Catherine, and Laura are playing a card game.

2. Paul is the dealer and deals the first card to his right.

3. Catherine gets the first card and Paul gets the last.

4. Laura, who is sitting across from Catherine, wins.

2. TRY-IT

Try-It is a new game, and the children love to play it. Where are the children sitting?

1. Joe Flow is Carol's partner.

2. Jill is Carol's brother's partner.

3. Daryl Barrel is Carol's brother.

4. Jill's last name is Mill.

5. Jill is sitting to the left of Joe.

3. ROUND-A-BOUT

On a hot summer day four children have nothing to do, so they make up a new game. The game requires that each child have a partner. In which order do the children sit around the table?

1. Mary always likes to sit to the right of a boy, and she does.

2. Trisha Jones and Joe decide to be partners.

3. Bobby always signs his name B. Krandall.

4. Mary and her sister Trisha really think that Round-A-Bout is a good name for the game.

5. Joe and his brother Bobby sleep in bunk beds.

4. TICKETS

Sandy Sanders, Marty Martin, Tommy Tucker, and Jason Jackson have invented a new complicated game called Tickets. Can you tell where each child sits?

1. The children always pass the tickets to the right.

2. Marty Martin passes his tickets to Tommy Tucker.

3. Jason Jackson and Marty Martin sit facing each other.

5. FAMILY AFFAIR

This is not a game. It is a serious family meeting. There are certain things that this family must discuss. Where does each person sit?

1. Dave Johnson sits next to Andy.

2. With his left hand, Eric accidentally bumps his sister, Karen, into Dave.

3. Eric Johnson is pleased with the meeting.

4. Andy is Dave's father.

6. THE CARD GAME

Every week, four people who work in the same office get together to play cards. On this particular evening, each player stays in the same seat for all the card games. Where does each person sit?

1. Tommy Towers and Linda are partners.

2. Ms. Thompson plays against Kelly and Mike.

3. Tommy and Mike are brothers.

4. Ms. Jones doesn't like Linda.

5. Linda is not sitting to Kelly's right.

7. TWINS

Bob and Rob are new children in town. They are also the only twins in town. Two girls ask the boys to come over to their house to play cards. The boys eagerly accept the invitation; they want to make new friends. Find out where each person sits.

1. As you already know, Bob and Rob are twins.

2. Kristine doesn't like Stacey too much, but she decides to be her partner.

3. Rob peeks at Ms. Teams' cards, so Stacey playfully slaps Rob across the shoulder with her left hand, without turning in her chair.

4. Bob Lob is keeping score because he has the best handwriting.

5. Ms. Kroft sits to the right of Bob.

8. FOUR BRIDGE PLAYERS

The same four women have played bridge each week for over 20 years. Although they have become very good friends, they still seem to enjoy arguing. Where do they sit for this particular game?

1. Annette doesn't like it when Ruth peeks at Annette's cards.

2. Ruth Barr and Miss Carson always argue.

3. Shirley gets mad because Annette keeps bumping her left elbow.

4. Mrs. Holmes has five children.

5. Jean thinks Annette is a great partner.

6. Except for Jean, all the women are married.

7. Mrs. Mays always plays with Miss Carson.

9. BACKPACKING

Four friends are planning a backpacking trip. John has a planning session at his house to decide who will share tents.

1. Ms. Trent is not John's mother, but her son is attending the planning session.

2. Jack is sitting on Jim's left and Jim is sitting next to John.

3. The Holt boy sits to the right of Jack.

4. Jack's last name is Dale, but the Stols boy is not Joe.

10. THREE SETS OF TWINS

The Snowman twins, Bowman twins, and Froman twins meet for their weekly game night. Where does each person sit, and what are their first names?

1. No sister sits next to her brother.

2. Sandy sits between Jane and Tom.

3. Jim Snowman sits between Betty and Fred.

4. Although Tom sits next to Mr. Froman, Ms. Froman sits next to Sandy.

5. Jane sits to the left of Betty.

11. ROYALTY

Prince Phillip, Prince James, Prince Charles, and Prince Andrew all decide to get together and talk about their countries' problems. Find out which country they are from and where they each sit. Put the princes' names on the top lines; put their countries' names on the bottom lines. (Don't bother about last names.)

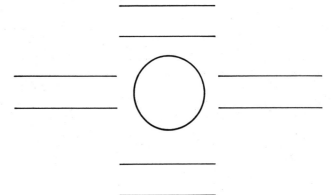

1. Prince Phillip does not remember ever meeting Prince James; they do not sit next to each other.

2. The prince from Denmark and the prince from England are very good friends, but they do not sit next to each other.

3. The prince from Luxembourg wants to know Prince Andrew better, so he sits next to him.

4. The prince from Monaco sits next to Prince Charles.

5. The prince from Denmark sits to the right of Prince James.

6. The prince from England sits across from Charles, but the prince from Luxembourg does not sit next to James.

12. NAMES

Ellen, Warren, Ruth, Elaine, and Rose have as last names Ellings, Wilson, Riley, East, and Ring (but not in that order).

1. No person's last name begins with the same letter as his or her first name.

2. The person with the last name of East sits to the right of the person with the last name of Ellings.

3. Ruth's last name is not Ellings.

4. Warren sits between Elaine and Ellen.

5. The person with the last name of Riley sits next to Rose.

6. Ellen's last name is not Wilson.

13. FAVORITE TV PROGRAMS

Six friends are discussing their favorite TV programs: "Little House on the Prairie," cartoons, "I Love Lucy," sports specials, news, and "That's Incredible." Find out each child's first name and his or her favorite TV program. Write children's names on the top lines, TV programs on the bottom lines.

1. The boy who likes sports specials sits directly to the right of Gordon.

2. Joel sits between the two people who watch "I Love Lucy" and sports specials.

3. No one sits between Bev and Kathy.

4. Kathy sits directly to the left of the boy who likes "Little House on the Prairie."

5. The boy who likes "That's Incredible" does not sit next to a girl.

6. Kathy does not care for cartoons.

7. Marty does not sit next to a girl.

8. Earl does not sit next to the girl who likes "I Love Lucy."

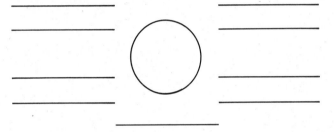

14. BOOK CLUB

Kate, Bill, Rhonda, Edna, Connie, Tim, and Sue have formed a new book club. You will need to know only the first names of the members. It will take a *lot* of logical thinking in order to find out where each person sits. Good luck!

1. Rhonda sits to the right of Edna.

2. Connie sits between Tim and Sue.

3. Bill sits next to Tim.

4. Kate sits next to Bill, but not next to Rhonda.

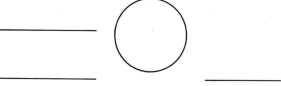

15. DINNER PARTY

Teri has a fancy dinner party for eight friends. Cindy, Judi, and Lyn don't sit next to any boys. Where does the hostess seat each of her eight guests?

1. John and Jeff sit next to each other.

2. Karen sits next to Miss Adams, and DeDe sits next to Paul.

3. Teri Moss enjoys sitting to the right of Jeff and also next to Paul.

4. The Thompson girl sits to the right of DeDe.

5. Judi Johnson sits between two girls.

6. Cindy does not sit next to Karen.

7. Paul and Jeff are twins.

8. The Beaver boys do not often see John.

9. The Fillmore girl sits to the right of the Adams girl.

10. The King girl is delighted to be invited to the gathering.

11. John and Judi are not related but do have the same last name.

*If you have trouble working this problem, be sure to reread the upper portion (situation) *very* carefully.

MAKE YOUR OWN TABLE LOGIC PROBLEMS

It's fun to create your own table logic problems! Here, the theme or story has been written for you. Children's names have been included in the diagram. Your job is to make up five questions or statements that will lead to the solution of where the children are sitting. Give your clues to a friend, and let him or her solve your problem.

BUBBLE-O

Four children are very excited about learning a new game called Bubble-O. Where does each child sit?

Frank
Foster

Myriam
Dowdy

Tina
Smith

Kevin
Thompson

Clues:

1. _____

2. _____

3. _____

4. _____

5. _____

MAKE YOUR OWN TABLE LOGIC PROBLEMS

For this problem, the story has been written for you. Your part is to make up your own names and enter them in the table diagram. Also, make up clues that will lead to the solution of where the children are sitting. Give your clues to a friend, and let him or her solve your problem.

MAGIC

Four friends are sitting around a table learning magic tricks. Where does each child sit?

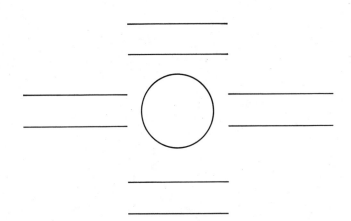

Clues:

1. _____

2. _____

3. _____

4. _____

5. _____

MAKE YOUR OWN TABLE LOGIC PROBLEM

First select a theme or story for your clues. Next, draw a table and fill in the names for your completed answer.

By referring to your completed table diagram, you can then make up clues that will lead to the solution of your problem.

In creating a table logic problem, you work in reverse of the way you would to solve one—by knowing the answers from the beginning.

MAKE UP A TABLE LOGIC PROBLEM HERE

Story:

Make diagram here:

Clues:

1. _____

2. _____

3. _____

4. _____

5. _____

CIRCLE LOGIC

Circle logic problems use circles. Each circle represents one group or category. The area where the circles overlap represents qualities common to all groups or categories. In the example below, label one circle *children*. Label the other circle *candy eaters*. The area where the two circles overlap shows children who eat candy.

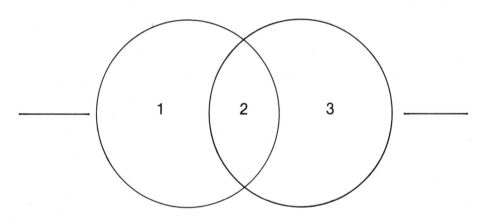

Here is another circle diagram.

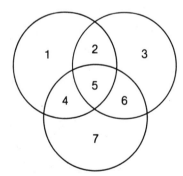

As you can see, it has three circles. The top two circles represent *children* and *candy eaters*. The bottom circle represents *males*. Each of the numbers represents a different area within the diagram. Circle logic problems always use three circles, and they are *always numbered just like this one.*

Now use the diagram to try some circle logic problems.

1. Where would a boy who does not eat candy be? (The boy is a child,

   so he'd be in the _____ circle. He is a male, so he'd be in

   ANSWER: Children.

   the _____ circle. He doesn't like candy, so he wouldn't

   ANSWER: Males.

   be in the _____ circle.

   ANSWER: Candy eaters.

   So a boy who does not eat candy would be inside the *children*
   circle, inside the *males* circle, but outside the *candy eaters* circle.
   Which number shows where only *children* and *males* overlap?

   _____ .)

   ANSWER: 4.

2. Where would a girl who doesn't eat candy be? (The girl is a child, so

   she'd be in the _____ circle. She is a female, so she

   ANSWER: Children.

   wouldn't be in the _____ circle. She doesn't eat

   ANSWER: Males.

   candy, so she wouldn't be in the _____ circle. She's only in

   ANSWER: Candy eaters.

   one circle. Which number shows where she is? _____ .)

   ANSWER: 1.

3. Where would a woman who eats candy be? (The woman is not a

   child, so she wouldn't be in the _____ circle. She is a

   ANSWER: Children.

   female, so she wouldn't be in the _____ circle. She eats

   ANSWER: Males.

   candy, so she would be in the _____ circle. She's only

   ANSWER: Candy eaters.

   in one circle. Which number shows where she is? _____ .)

   ANSWER: 3.

Copyright © 1982

4. Where would a boy who eats candy be? (The boy is a child, so he'd

be in the _____ circle. He is a male, so he'd be in the

ANSWER: Children.

_____ circle. He eats candy, so he'd be in the

ANSWER: Males.

_____ circle. Which number shows where those three

ANSWER: Candy eaters.

circles overlap? _____ .)

ANSWER: 5.

5. Where would a girl who eats candy be? (The girl is a child, so she'd

be in the _____ circle. She eats candy, so she'd be in the

ANSWER: Children.

_____ circle. She's a female, so she wouldn't be

ANSWER: Candy eaters.

in the _____ circle. She's in two circles. What number

ANSWER: Males.

shows where those circles overlap? _____ .)

ANSWER: 2.

6. Where would a man who doesn't eat candy be? (The man is a male,

so he'd be in the _____ circle. He doesn't eat candy, so he

ANSWER: Males.

wouldn't be in the _____ circle. He isn't a child, so he

ANSWER: Candy eaters.

wouldn't be in the _____ circle. He's only in one circle.

ANSWER: Children.

What number shows where he is? _____ .)

ANSWER: 7.

7. Where would a man who eats candy be? (He is a male, so he'd be

in the _____ circle. He isn't a child, so he wouldn't be in the

ANSWER: Males.

the _____ circle. He eats candy, so he'd be in the

ANSWER: Children.

_____ circle. He's in two circles. What number

ANSWER: Candy eaters.

shows where those two circles overlap? _____ .)

ANSWER: 6.

Now, practice labeling a circle diagram correctly.
Label the circle on the left "children."
Label the circle on the right "candy eaters."
Label the circle on the bottom "males."
Number the parts of the circle 1–7 starting with the circle on the left.
(Check your numbering with the Circle Logic Reminder Page.)

CIRCLE LOGIC REMINDER PAGE

- Make all circles large and round.

- Draw the three circles so they will overlap.

- Label the circles by placing the *first category on the left,* the *second category on the right,* and the *third category at the bottom.*

- The area where the circles overlap represents attributes or qualities of both groups or categories.

- Number the circles correctly, beginning with #1 at the top left, #2 at the top center, #3 at the top right, and so on. #7 is the bottom circle.

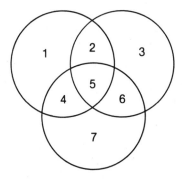

- Always make circle diagrams *exactly this way.*

1. DRINKS

Cola, orange soda, and *milk* are popular drinks liked by many children. In which area of the circles would each child stand?

1. Barbara drinks only cola and milk. _____

2. Kathy will drink any kind of beverage. _____

3. John drinks only milk. _____

4. Tim likes orange soda and milk but does not care for colas.

_____

5. Bill says, "Orange drinks are the only thing for me." _____

Make diagram here

2. SCHOOL GRADES

In which areas of the circles would you place these children? The categories are *A, B,* and *C.*

1. Jill always gets A's in school. _____

2. Bill has never earned an A, but he also has never received a C or

lower. _____

3. Last semester, Julie received two A's, three B's, and two C's.

_____

4. Fred is an A and B student only. _____

5. Brenda always gets C's but tries her hardest in all her classes.

_____

Make diagram here

3. READING TASTES

Place the *mystery* readers, the *comedy* readers, and the *science fiction* readers in the correct areas.

1. Mrs. Fee likes to read anything except cartoons. _____

2. Mrs. Tee likes to read only funny, happy books. _____

3. Mr. Dee will read any book that he can get his hands on.

_____

4. Ms. Hee confines her reading to science fiction only. _____

Make diagram here

4. CARS

Fords, *Chevrolets*, and *Volkswagens* are popular cars. Show where each of the following people belong by entering the correct numeral (from the area of the circles) in the blank.

1. Mr. Smith never bought a car that wasn't made by Ford.

_____

2. Mrs. Jones can't think of a car that she hasn't owned. _____

3. Freddie thinks Chevies are the only cars to drive—he hasn't owned

any other kind. _____

4. Donna just bought her first car and chose a VW. _____

Make diagram here

5. SUMMER FUN

Skateboards, roller skates, and *bikes* are used at the recreation center park. Fill in the correct area numeral for each group.

1. The girls will use any equipment that has wheels. _____

2. The boys have only roller skate and skateboard races.

   _____

3. The members of the "Mothers' Club" limit themselves to bikes.

   _____

4. The members of the "Grandpa Group" have started a skateboard club, and that's the only sport in which they will participate.

   _____

5. The "Tiny Tots" are all learning to roller skate. _____

Make diagram here

6. SCHOOL SUBJECTS

Into which area of the circles do the following children fit? The categories are: *math, reading,* and *science.*

1. Bill loves reading, and that's all. _____

2. Laureen loves all her classes. _____

3. Joe likes all his classes except math. _____

4. Rhonda likes science and math but doesn't care for any other subject. _____

5. Tom does not have one class that he likes. _____

Make diagram here

7. ARE YOU HUNGRY?

The categories in this problem are *sweets, vegetables,* and *cereals*. Into which areas of the circles do the following children fit?

1. Bill is a vegetarian. _____

2. Mary will eat anything except vegetables. _____

3. There is nothing that Derek doesn't eat. _____

4. Don likes sweets but he will also eat cereals. _____

5. Tom has given up eating sweets but he will eat anything else.

_____

Make diagram here

8. MUSIC, MUSIC, MUSIC

Place the correct numeral, from the circles, on the lines to show which musical instrument or instruments each person plays. Your choices are the *flute, French Horn,* and *violin.*

1. Marcia can play any musical instrument. _____

2. Tim plays any instrument that does not require him to use his mouth.

_____

3. Wayne can play only curved horns. _____

4. Beverly has just learned to play her first instrument, and it has

strings. _____

Make diagram here

9. GARDENS

Several neighborhood families plant their own backyard gardens. Each family decides what *flowers, vegetables,* or *fruit trees* to plant. Into which areas do these gardens fit?

1. The Jones family plants only vegetables. _____

2. The Whites plant apples and artichokes. _____

3. Debbie, the Whites' daughter, plants her own garden with carrots and apricots. _____

4. The Fields love flowers, and that is what they plant. _____

5. Cherries and flowers are the Stones' favorites. _____

6. The Bowels have a prize rose garden. _____

7. Vegetables, flowers, and a lemon tree are planted by the Garcias.

   _____

8. The Itos use only fresh vegetables from their garden and raise prize tulips as a hobby. _____

Make diagram here

10. SOFT, WHITE, AND FURRY

In what areas of the circles would you place the following things? The categories are *soft, white,* and *furry.*

1. Bunny _____
2. Marshmallow _____
3. Pearl _____
4. Snow _____
5. Orange _____
6. Rice _____
7. Chalk _____
8. Polar bear _____
9. Cotton _____
10. Black kitten _____

Make diagram here

MAKE YOUR OWN CIRCLE LOGIC PROBLEM

Here is a problem that's already started for you. To complete the problem, make up five statements that will fit into one, two, or all of the categories.

THE COLLECTORS

Boys and girls everywhere enjoy collecting *stamps, coins,* and *records* as a hobby. In what areas of the circles do these collectors stand?

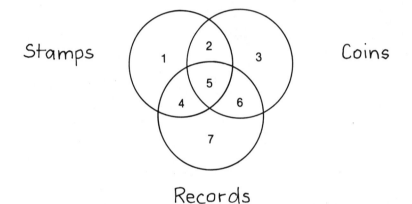

1. Jeff has a collection of the Beatles. _____

2. _____

3. _____

4. _____

5. _____

6. _____

MAKE YOUR OWN CIRCLE LOGIC PROBLEM

In this problem, the title, introduction, and categories are here for you to work with. Your task is to diagram the problem and write five or more statements.

GAMES KIDS PLAY

Baseball, tennis, and *kickball* are fun to play. In which areas of the circles would these kids stand?

Make diagram here

1. _____
2. _____
3. _____
4. _____
5. _____

MAKE YOUR OWN CIRCLE LOGIC PROBLEM

To begin, make three interlocking circles. Give each circle a category. Number the areas of the circles. Now make up statements that will fit into one, two, or all of the categories. To complete your problem, write an introduction and give it a catchy title.

SYLLOGISMS

In ancient Greece, the philosopher Aristotle challenged his students with logic problems called *syllogisms.* A syllogism has three parts, and must be worded in a particular way. Here's an example:

> All dogs are barking animals.
> All poodles are dogs.
> Therefore, all poodles are barking animals.

The first line gives you one piece of information—all dogs are barking animals. The second line gives you another piece of information—all poodles are dogs. Each of the first two statements in a syllogism is called a *premise.*

You put the information from the premises together to get the *conclusion.* The conclusion is the third statement in a syllogism.

If the conclusion is supported or proved by the information in the premises, the syllogism is *valid.*

If the conclusion is not supported or proved by the information in the premises, the syllogism is *invalid.*

Is the syllogism about dogs, barking animals, and poodles valid or

invalid? _____

ANSWER: Valid.

Here's another syllogism using dogs, barking animals, and poodles:

> All poodles are dogs.
> All poodles are barking animals.
> Therefore, all dogs are barking animals.

From the first premise you know that _____.

ANSWER: All poodles are dogs.

From the second premise you know that _____.

ANSWER: All poodles are barking animals.

But when you put the information from the two premises together, you still don't have enough information to conclude anything about *all dogs.* There may be some dogs that are not poodles, and there's no information about them here. The two premises do not support or prove

the conclusion. So this syllogism is _____.

ANSWER: Invalid.

The three statements in this type of logic problem are called an *argument*. It's not the kind of argument in which people disagree with each other. It is the kind of argument in which a *conclusion* is supported by two *premises*.

There are three different categories, or *sets*, in a syllogism. In the syllogism about the dogs, the three sets are *dogs, barking animals,* and *poodles.*

It is a rule of syllogisms that each statement must contain two of the three sets.

It is also a rule of syllogisms that each set must be used only twice. What are the sets?

All dogs are barking animals: _____ and _____ .

ANSWER: Dogs; barking animals.

All poodles are dogs: _____ and _____ .

ANSWER: Poodles; dogs.

Therefore, all poodles are barking animals: _____ and

_____ .

ANSWER: Poodles; barking animals.

What are the sets in this syllogism?

All flowers are pretty: _____ and _____ .

ANSWER: Flowers; pretty.

All daffodils are flowers: _____ and _____ .

ANSWER: Daffodils; flowers.

Therefore, all daffodils are pretty: _____ and _____ .

ANSWER: Daffodils; pretty.

Is this a valid syllogism? _____

ANSWER: Yes.

It is valid. The first premise says that all flowers are pretty. The second premise says that all daffodils are flowers. Since daffodils are flowers and all flowers are pretty, daffodils must be pretty.

Let's change the syllogism a little:

All flowers are pretty.
All daffodils are pretty.
Therefore, all daffodils are flowers.

The first premise tells us that _____ .

ANSWER: All flowers are pretty.

The second premise tells us that _____.

When we fit those two pieces of information together, can we come

to the conclusion that "all daffodils are flowers"? _____

The answer is no. The two premises together don't give any
information about all daffodils being flowers, or flowers being daffodils.
The conclusion doesn't follow logically from the premises.

But you know that daffodils *are* flowers, don't you? You're right—but
here is something very important to remember about syllogisms:

It doesn't matter whether the information is true or false. What
matters is whether or not the conclusion follows logically from the
premises.

Here is a syllogism that seems quite silly. None of the statements is
true. But the syllogism is *valid* because the conclusion follows logically
from the premises:

> All dogs have three legs.
> All ducks are dogs.
> Therefore, all ducks have three legs.

The wording of syllogisms is important. The two premises usually
begin with the words *all, no,* or *some.* The premises usually contain the
words *is, are,* or *are not.* The conclusion always begins with the word
therefore.

When both the premises begin with the word *all,* the conclusion
must contain the word *all:*

> *All* dragons are green.
> *All* green things are ugly.
> Therefore, *all* dragons are ugly.

When one of the premises begins with the word *no* or *nothing,* the
conclusion must contain the word *no* or *nothing:*

> *No* crooks are honest.
> All burglars are crooks.
> Therefore, *no* burglars are honest.

When one of the premises uses the word *some,* the conclusion must
use the word *some:*

> All vegetables taste good.
> *Some* foods are vegetables.
> Therefore, *some* foods taste good.

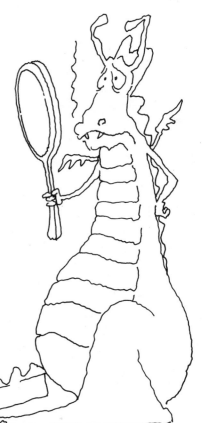

In syllogisms with conclusions that say, "no _____ are _____," or "some _____ are _____," you can *reverse the sets in the conclusions.* Here's an example:

All fur coats are warm.
No bathing suits are warm.
Therefore, no bathing suits are fur coats.

Or

Therefore, no fur coats are bathing suits.

Here's another:

All candies are sweets.
Some candies are chocolates.
Therefore, some chocolates are sweets.

Or

Therefore, some sweets are chocolates.

Here are five syllogisms for you to complete by adding conclusions:

All children are TV watchers.
No TV watchers are pigs.

Therefore, _____ are _____ .

ANSWER: No children are pigs. Or, no pigs are children.

All carrots are vegetables.
All vegetables are nutritious.

Therefore, _____ are _____ .

ANSWER: All carrots are nutritious.

No human beings are fish.
All trout are fish.

Therefore, _____ are _____ .

ANSWER: No human beings are trout. Or, no trout are human beings.

Some good students are girls.
All good students are hard workers.

Therefore, _____ are _____ .

ANSWER: Some girls are hard workers. Or, some hard workers are girls.

All rabbits are furry animals.
No furry animals are snails.

Therefore, _____ are _____ .

ANSWER: No rabbits are snails. Or, no snails are rabbits.

SYLLOGISM REMINDER PAGE

- A syllogism is made up of three sentences or statements.

- The three sentences or statements are referred to as an *argument*.

- The first two statements in a syllogism are called *premises*.

- The third sentence in a syllogism is called the *conclusion*.

- The two premises contain clues that support or prove the conclusion.

- A syllogism always contains three different categories or *sets*.

- Each set *must* appear in two of the three statements; each set is used twice in a syllogism.

- Syllogisms are worded in a special way.
Premises begin with "all," "no," or "some"; they use the verbs "is," "are," or "are not." A conclusion begins with the word "therefore."

- It is not important whether or not the premises are true or whether they make sense. This is because many times you do not (or cannot) know whether the premises are true or false. Your only concern is that the two premises *do* prove the conclusion.

- If a conclusion follows logically from the two premises or is supported by the two premises, an argument is said to be *valid*.

- If a conclusion does not follow logically from the two premises or is not supported by the two premises, an argument is said to be *invalid*.

Mark the syllogisms *valid* or *invalid.*

1. All bears have fur.
All Kodiaks are bears.
Therefore, all Kodiaks have fur. _____

2. All books are big.
All trees are big.
Therefore, all books are trees. _____

3. All lemons are yellow.
No cherries are yellow.
Therefore, no cherries are lemons. _____

4. Some pink things grow.
All flowers grow.
Therefore, some pink things are flowers. _____

5. All newspapers are written in type.
No books are newspapers.
Therefore, no books are written in type. _____

6. Some toys are durable.
All durable objects are desirable.
Therefore, some toys are desirable. _____

7. All pillows are soft.
All soft things are comfortable.
Therefore, all pillows are comfortable. _____

8. No dogs are small.
All dogs are cute.
Therefore, nothing small is cute. _____

9. All paper is thin.
All thin things are flimsy.
Therefore, all flimsy things are paper. _____

10. All fire is hot.
Nothing hot is cold.
Therefore, no fire is cold. _____

11. Some growing things are grass.
All green things grow.
Therefore, some grass is green. _____

12. All tomatoes are red.
All red things are edible.
Therefore, all tomatoes are edible. _____

VENN DIAGRAMS

You can test whether a syllogism is valid or invalid by using a *Venn Diagram*. Named after the man who devised it, John Venn, this diagram uses three overlapping circles. Each circle represents one of the three categories or sets in the syllogism. Here is an example:

All flowers are pretty.
All daffodils are flowers.
Therefore, all daffodils are pretty.

This circle represents flowers (areas 1, 2, 4 and 5)

This circle represents things that are pretty (areas 2, 3, 5 and 6)

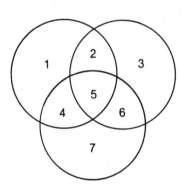

This circle represents daffodils (areas 4, 5, 6 and 7)

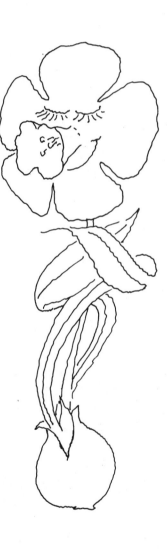

The first premise, *all flowers are pretty,* means that there are no members of the *flower* set that are not in the *pretty* set. To show this on the Venn Diagram below, shade in all of the circle representing flowers that doesn't overlap the circle representing pretty things. The shading in means that there is *nothing* in that portion of the circle.

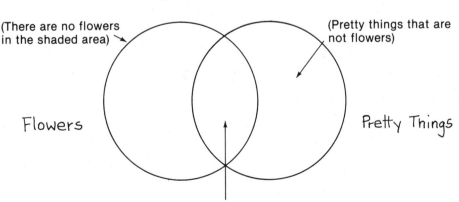

(There are no flowers in the shaded area) →

(Pretty things that are not flowers)

Flowers

Pretty Things

(Flowers that are pretty)

The second premise is: *All daffodils are flowers.* Look at the two circles representing *daffodils* and *flowers.* There are no daffodils that are not flowers. Shade in all the *daffodil* circle that is outside the *flower* circle (areas 6 and 7).

 Flowers 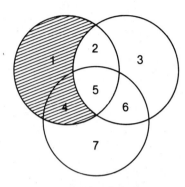 Pretty Things

1 2 3
5
4 6
7

Daffodils

Look at the conclusion: *Therefore, all daffodils are pretty.* Now look at the diagram. Remember that the shaded-in part of the *daffodil* circle has no daffodils. So *all* daffodils are in area number _____.

ANSWER: 5.

What circles overlap in that area? _____, _____, and _____.

ANSWER: Flowers; pretty things; daffodils.

Since all daffodils are in area number 5, is the conclusion, *All daffodils are pretty,* valid or invalid? _____

ANSWER: Valid.

Here's another one to try:

All dogs are apple eaters.
All apple eaters are mammals.
Therefore, all dogs are mammals.

What three sets do the circles represent? _____,

_____, and _____.

ANSWER: Dogs; apple eaters; mammals.

Label the circles:

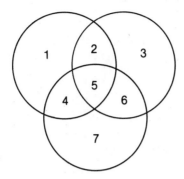

First premise: *All dogs are apple eaters.* Shade in the area of the *dogs* circle that doesn't overlap with the *apple eaters* circle. (Since all dogs eat apples, there are no dogs that are not apple eaters.)

Next, shade in the area in the *apple eaters* circle that doesn't overlap with the *mammals* circle. (Since all apple eaters are mammals, there are no apple eaters that aren't mammals.)

Your diagram should now look like this:

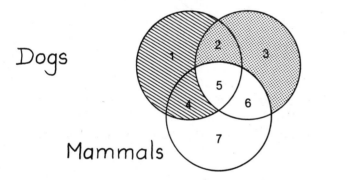

Look at the conclusion: *All dogs are mammals.* Now look at the diagram. Remember that there are no dogs in the shaded areas. All

dogs are in area number _____ .

ANSWER: 5.

The circles that overlap in that area are _____ ,

_____ , and _____ .

ANSWER: Dogs; apple eaters; mammals.

Is the conclusion, *All dogs are mammals,* valid or invalid?

_____

ANSWER: Valid.

As you know, statements can use the words *no* and *some*. These statements also can be diagrammed, but in a different way. Let's take a look at a syllogism using the word "no."

All men are human beings.
No human beings have three legs.
Therefore, no men have three legs.

First premise: *All men are human beings.* Shade in all of the *men* circle that is *not* in the *human beings* circle. This shading will show that there are no men in the areas of the circle who are not human beings. All the men are in the human beings circle.

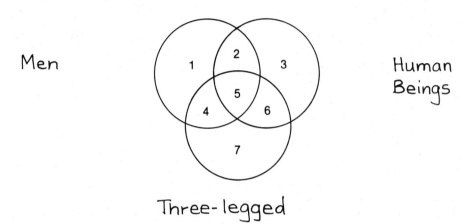

Second premise: *No human beings have three legs.* Shade in the portion of the circle where the *human beings* circle and the *three-legged* circle overlap. This will show that there are no human beings who have three legs. *The shading shows that these areas are empty.*

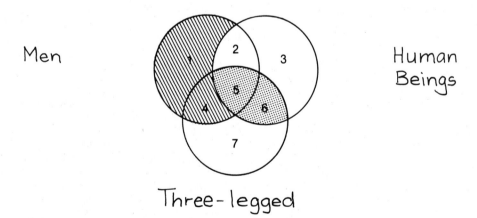

Conclusion: Therefore, *no men have three legs.* Look at the two circles that show *men* and *three legs* (areas 4 and 5). Notice that the spaces where the two circles overlap have been all shaded in. Now look at the portion of the *men* circle that is not shaded in (area 2). Area 2 is outside of the *three-legged* circle. This shows that there are not any men in the three-legged area. This is what the conclusion says: *No men have three legs.* The two premises support the conclusion. The syllogism is valid.

When diagramming statements using the word *some,* use an asterisk (*). An asterisk can show that there is at least one member of a set that is *not* included in another set.

For example:

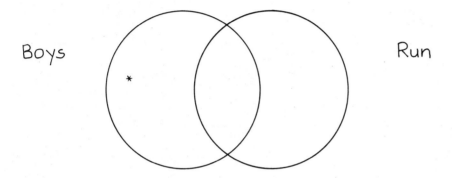

The asterisk shows
that there are some boys
who *do not* run.

An asterisk can also show that there is at least one member of a set that *is* included in another set. Place an asterisk in the area where the circles overlap.

Example:

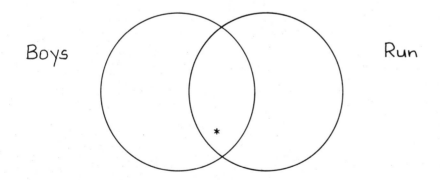

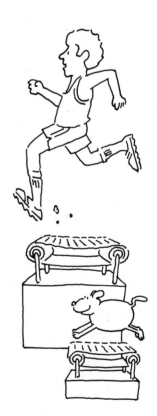

The asterisk shows
that there are some boys
who *do* run.

Important: *Do not place an asterisk in a shaded area.*

The following syllogism requires you to diagram *some*.

All children go to school
Some good students are children.
Therefore, some good students go to school.

First premise: *All children go to school.* Shade in the area of the *children* circle that is not within the *school* circle (areas 1 and 4).

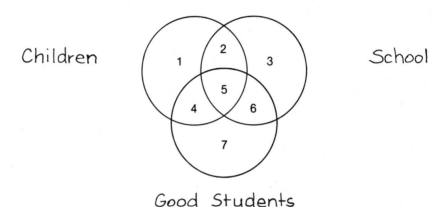

Second premise: *Some good students are children.* Put an asterisk in the area where the *good students* and *children* circles overlap (area 5). The asterisk shows that there is at least one good student who is a child. Remember, *do not put an asterisk in a shaded area.*

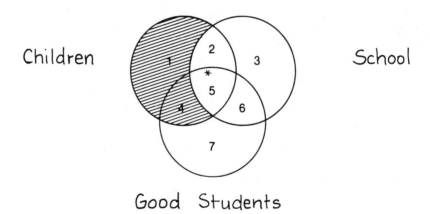

Conclusion: *Some good students go to school.* Look at where the *good student* and *school* circles overlap. The asterisk shows that there is at least one good student who goes to school.

When diagramming a syllogism that has one premise beginning with "some" and another premise beginning with "all" or "no," first diagram the premise that begins with "no" or "all." Otherwise, you wouldn't know exactly which areas of the circle to put the asterisk in.

If you don't know in which areas to place an asterisk in order to show the premise "some," enter two asterisks and join them with a line. This will always show that the syllogism is *invalid.* For example:

Some wheels are large.
All cars have wheels.
Some large things are cars.

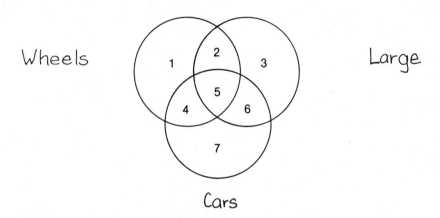

Remember to diagram the *all* and *no* sentences before you do the *some* sentences. Shade in areas 6 and 7 to show that *all cars have wheels* (there are no cars that do not have wheels). Next, put an asterisk to show that there are some wheels that are large. Into which area would you place it? That's right—you wouldn't know! You could put it in area 2 or in area 5. So place an asterisk in both areas and join them with a straight line. This syllogism is invalid because you don't know where the asterisk belongs.

VENN DIAGRAM REMINDER PAGE

- A Venn Diagram proves a syllogism *valid* or *invalid*.

- A Venn Diagram consists of three overlapping circles representing the three categories of a syllogism.

- Each circle is labeled for a different category or subject in a syllogism.

- Diagram one premise at a time, looking only at two overlapping circles that represent the sets in each premise.

- Shading in a portion of a circle means that there is nothing left in that area. In other words, that portion is empty.

- When diagramming a syllogism containing one premise beginning with *some* and another premise beginning with *all* or *no,* shade in the *all* or *no* premise first.

- In syllogisms using the word *some,* an asterisk (*) can show that there is at least one member of a set that *is* included in another set. An asterisk can also show that there is at least one member of a set that *is not* included in another set.

- Do not place an asterisk in an area that has been shaded in.

- If you don't have enough information to know where to place an asterisk when diagramming the premise *some,* put an asterisk in each area and join the asterisks with a line. Syllogisms containing joined asterisks are always *invalid.*

- When reading a Venn Diagram for validity, look only at the two circles representing the two categories in the conclusion.

- A syllogism is valid if the diagram shows exactly what the conclusion says.

For each syllogism, draw a Venn Diagram in the space provided. Use the diagram to prove whether the syllogism is valid or invalid. Write your answer in the blank.

1. All pigs are red.
All red things are cute.
Therefore, all pigs are cute. _____

Make diagram here

2. All trees are green.
All pines are trees.
Therefore, all pines are green. _____

Make diagram here

For each syllogism, draw a Venn Diagram in the space provided. Use the diagram to prove whether the syllogism is valid or invalid. Write your answer in the blank.

3. All cats are animals.
No animals are plants.
Therefore, no cat is a plant. _____

Make diagram here

4. All boys have two legs.
All human beings have two legs.
Therefore, all boys are humans. _____

Make diagram here

For each syllogism, draw a Venn Diagram in the space provided. Use the diagram to prove whether the syllogism is valid or invalid. Write your answer in the blank.

5. All S is M.
All M is P.
Therefore, all S is P. _____

Make diagram here

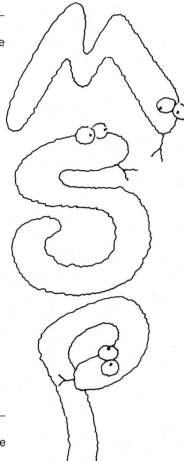

6. All teachers are smart.
All nice people are smart.
Therefore, all nice people are teachers. _____

Make diagram here

For each syllogism, draw a Venn Diagram in the space provided. Use the diagram to prove whether the syllogism is valid or invalid. Write your answer in the blank.

7. All red hair is pretty.
No pretty things are dull.
Therefore, no red hair is dull. _____

Make diagram here

8. All geometry is difficult.
No algebra is geometry.
Therefore, no algebra is difficult. _____

Make diagram here

For each syllogism, draw a Venn Diagram in the space provided. Use the diagram to prove whether the syllogism is valid or invalid. Write your answer in the blank.

9. All good students are good readers.
Some good math students are good students.
Therefore, some good math students are good readers. _____

Make diagram here

10. All students are human beings.
Some boys are students.
Therefore, some human beings are boys. _____

Make diagram here

For each syllogism, draw a Venn Diagram in the space provided. Use the diagram to prove whether the syllogism is valid or invalid. Write your answer in the blank.

11. All Bongs are Wongs.
    Some Tongs are Bongs.
    Therefore, some Tongs are Wongs. _____

Make diagram here

12. No human beings are snakes.
    All human beings are mammals.
    Therefore, no snakes are mammals. _____

Make diagram here

For each syllogism, draw a Venn Diagram in the space provided. Use the diagram to prove whether the syllogism is valid or invalid. Write your answer in the blank.

13. All mice are small.
Nothing small is large.
Therefore, no mice are large. _____

Make diagram here

14. All glass is breakable.
Some breakable objects are expensive.
Therefore, some glass is expensive. _____

Make diagram here

For each syllogism, draw a Venn Diagram in the space provided. Use the diagram to prove whether the syllogism is valid or invalid. Write your answer in the blank.

15. All artists are creative people.
Some musicians are artists.
Therefore, some musicians are creative people. _____

Make diagram here

16. All squares are rectangles.
All rectangles are quadrilateral.
Therefore, all squares are quadrilateral. _____

Make diagram here

For each syllogism, draw a Venn Diagram in the space provided. Use the diagram to prove whether the syllogism is valid or invalid. Write your answer in the blank.

17. All cars have engines.
Some engines are gas users.
Therefore, some cars are gas users. _____

Make diagram here

18. No hamsters have horns.
Some furry animals are hamsters.
Therefore, some furry animals do not have horns. _____

Make diagram here

For each syllogism, draw a Venn Diagram in the space provided. Use the diagram to prove whether the syllogism is valid or invalid. Write your answer in the blank.

19. All bugabears are weird.
All Orcs are bugabears.
Therefore, all weird things are Orcs. _____

Make diagram here

20. No apples are dapples.
All yapples are apples.
Therefore, no dapples are yapples. _____

Make diagram here

MAKE YOUR OWN SYLLOGISMS AND VENN DIAGRAMS

It is quite simple to create your own syllogisms when using the Venn Diagram. Remember: When both premises begin with the word *all,* the conclusion must also contain the word *all.* When one of the premises begins with the word *no* or *nothing,* the conclusion must also contain these words. When one of the premises uses the word *some,* the conclusion must also use the word *some.*

The syllogism below has been started for you. After reading it, you will know what categories you need for the conclusion. However, you do not know the correct order in which to place the categories to make the syllogism *valid.*

Draw a Venn Diagram. Label and number it. By diagramming the two premises, you can see the correct order for the sets in the conclusion. Write the sets on the lines.

All friendly people are likeable.

All likeable people are popular.

Therefore, all _____ are _____ .

Make diagram here

ANSWERS: Friendly people; popular.

MAKE YOUR OWN SYLLOGISMS
AND VENN DIAGRAMS

Here a syllogism has been started for you. The three categories are: *chickens, fowls,* and *dogs.* Draw a Venn Diagram next to this problem. Make the syllogism valid.

All chickens are fowls.

No fowls are _____ .

Therefore, no _____ are _____ .

Make diagram here

ANSWERS: The word *dogs* would complete the second premise. The conclusion would read either "no *dogs* are *chickens*" or "no *chickens* are *dogs*."

Complete the following syllogism using the word "some." The categories are: *children, curious,* and *cats.* Make the syllogism and Venn Diagram invalid.

All children are curious.

Some curious things are _____ .

Therefore, some _____ are _____ .

Make diagram here

ANSWERS: The second premise would contain the word *cat.* The conclusion would read: "some *children* are *cats*" or "some *cats* are *children*." The syllogism would be invalid because you would not know exactly where to place the asterisk when diagramming the second premise.

MAKE YOUR OWN SYLLOGISMS
AND VENN DIAGRAMS

Using a completed Venn Diagram will make it easy for you to create a syllogism.

    First, think up three categories. Then draw a Venn Diagram; label it and add the numerals. Complete the diagram before you write the syllogism. This is a way to make up very difficult (also very tricky) syllogisms. Good luck!

All _____ is/are _____.

No _____ is/are _____.

Therefore, no _____ is/are _____.

Make diagram here

All _____ is/are _____.

Some _____ is/are _____.

Therefore, some _____ is/are _____.

Make diagram here

Mark the syllogisms *valid* or *invalid*. Test your answers using Venn Diagrams.

1. All gold is expensive.
   Some rings are gold.
   Therefore, some rings are expensive. _____

2. All books have pages.
   Some books are novels.
   Therefore, some novels have pages. _____

3. All taffy is sticky.
   Some sticky things are yucky.
   Therefore, some taffy is yucky. _____

4. All dragons are green.
   All green things are ugly.
   Therefore, all dragons are ugly. _____

5. All children like to play.
   All girls are children.
   Therefore, all girls like to play. _____

6. All fragile things are breakable.
   Some mirrors are fragile.
   Therefore, some mirrors are breakable. _____

7. All zebras have stripes.
   No zebras are polar bears.
   Therefore, no polar bears have stripes. _____

8. No ship is safe.
   All ships are large.
   Therefore, no large things are safe. _____

9. All men are smart.
   All smart things are small.
   Therefore, all men are small. _____

10. All butterflies have wings.
    All flies have wings.
    Therefore, all butterflies are flies. _____

11. All motorcycles have two wheels.
    Some motorcycles are fast.
    Therefore, some two-wheeled things are fast. _____

12. All clowns are funny.
    Some happy people are clowns.
    Therefore, some happy people are funny. _____

Mark the syllogisms *valid* or *invalid.* Test your answers using Venn Diagrams.

13. All rocks are heavy.
    Some hard things are rocks.
    Therefore, some hard things are heavy. _____

14. All masks are scary.
    Some noises are scary.
    Therefore, some masks are noises. _____

15. Some youngsters are good athletes.
    All baseball players are good athletes.
    Therefore, some youngsters are baseball players. _____

16. All boats are metal.
    All metal is strong.
    Therefore, all strong things are boats. _____

17. Some boats float.
    All floating things are fast.
    Therefore, some boats are fast. _____

18. All triangles have three sides.
    No three-sided things are squares.
    Therefore, no triangles are squares. _____

19. All flags can wave.
    Some flags are red.
    Therefore, some red things can wave. _____

20. Nothing that spins is square.
    All tops are spinning objects.
    Therefore, no top is square. _____

21. Some lights are bright.
    All bright things shine.
    Therefore, some things that shine are lights. _____

22. All movies are neat.
    Some scary things are movies.
    Therefore, some neat things are scary. _____

23. All dogs are barking animals.
    All cute things are dogs.
    Therefore, all barking animals are cute. _____

24. All presidents are small.
    All small people are brave.
    Therefore, all presidents are brave. _____

Mark the syllogisms *valid* or *invalid*. Test your answers using Venn Diagrams.

25. All bears are mammals.
All humans are mammals.
Therefore, all bears are humans. _____

26. All R are D.
No R are W.
Therefore, no W are D. _____

27. Some dogs cannot fly.
All hawks can fly.
Therefore, some dogs are not hawks. _____

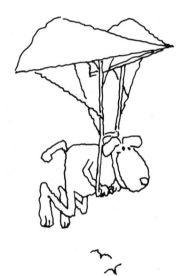

28. All deeples are keeples.
All keeples are beeps.
Therefore, all deeples are beeps. _____

29. All radios are loud.
All big things are loud.
Therefore, all big things are radios. _____

30. All sincere people are dependable.
No dependable people are dishonest.
Therefore, no sincere people are dishonest. _____

31. All planets are high.
All big things are high.
Therefore, all planets are big things. _____

32. Some striges are soft.
All zombies are striges.
Therefore, some soft things are zombies. _____

33. All busses are big.
Some big things are yellow.
Therefore, some busses are yellow. _____

34. All boxes are six-sided.
All six-sided things are hollow.
Therefore, all boxes are hollow. _____

35. All misers are frugal people.
No frugal people are extravagant.
Therefore, no misers are extravagant. _____

36. All giants are tall.
Some people are tall.
Therefore, some giants are people. _____

Mark the syllogisms *valid* or *invalid*. Test your answers using Venn Diagrams.

37. All rain is wet.
No rain is dry.
Therefore, nothing dry is wet. _____

38. No chairs have two legs.
All chairs are standing objects.
Therefore, no two-legged things are standing objects.

_____

39. No flowers are ugly.
All flowers can bloom.
Therefore, nothing that blooms is ugly. _____

40. All goblins are ghosts.
No goblins are werewolves.
Therefore, no werewolves are ghosts. _____

41. All cats are curious.
All green things are curious.
Therefore, all green things are cats. _____

42. All monsters are fierce.
All fierce things are purple.
Therefore, all purple things are monsters. _____

43. All gnomes are green.
Some green things are Oagles.
Therefore, some gnomes are Oagles. _____

44. All silver is valuable.
No valuable things are inexpensive.
Therefore, no silver is inexpensive. _____

45. All dodos are extinct.
No dinosaurs are dodos.
Therefore, no dinosaurs are extinct. _____

46. All dungeons have traps.
Some traps are dangerous.
Therefore, some dungeons are dangerous. _____

47. No kings are elected.
Some presidents are elected.
Therefore, some presidents are not kings. _____

48. No X are Z.
All Z are Y.
Therefore, no Y are X. _____

ANSWER KEY

Analogies

1. day
2. mad
3. air
4. heat
5. hat
6. more
7. wide
8. air
9. hair
10. many
11. bone
12. compass
13. wall
14. car
15. body
16. bandit
17. car
18. cockpit
19. sister
20. people
21. freezing
22. night
23. color
24. butterfly
25. bread
26. car
27. envelope
28. molding
29. carrot
30. string
31. eat
32. smell
33. shell
34. pen
35. barn
36. mallet
37. tee
38. body
39. fruit
40. language
41. Oregon
42. food
43. mountain
44. odometer
45. hare
46. aqueduct
47. difference
48. view
49. Saturday
50. talk

Matrix Logic

HOUSES, BOYS, AND PETS

	House Color				Location (white house)				Pet			
	Brown	White	Green	Blue	First	Second	Third	Fourth	Worm	Bear	Gorilla	Bull
Billy Brown										X		X
Willie White						X			X	X	X	yes
George Green					X				X	yes	X	X
Bobby Blue										X		X

1. Flowers

Karen—roses
Derek—daisies
Fay—violets
Tanya—tulips
Scott—carnations

2. The Artists

Mark—water colors
Meg—felt pens
Melissa—crayons
Marcie—black pencils

3. Cleaning Day

Darla—bedroom
Connie—bathroom
Jay—living room
Troy—den
Phil—kitchen

4. Family Vacation

Lake Z—swimming
Lake F—hiking
Lake S—fishing
Lake R—camping

5. Piano Lessons

Betty—9:00
Bob—3:00
Brenda—5:00

6. Who Lives Where?

Cathy —orange house
—Maple
Brian —brown house
—Lake Street
Joann —red house
—Anza Avenue

7. Find the Sport

Joe—hockey
Donna—kickball
Denise—soccer
Kent—football
Scott—baseball

8. Careers

Don—house painter—30 years
Robert—teacher—22 years
Laura—plumber—25 years

9. R.I.P.

Fred—first
Tony—second
Robert—third
Bill—fourth
John—fifth
Jack—sixth

10. This Is Not Easy

Sean—red house—2
Julie—blue house—11
Kim—blue house—4
Mary—white house—17
Ted—black house—6

11. Circus Time

Jimmy—camel—snow cone
Amy—tiger—cotton candy
Bob—zebra—ice cream
Tracy—lion—popcorn

12. Birthday Parties

Lisa—Sunday
Pat—Monday
Sandy—Tuesday
Jennifer—Wednesday
Jim—Thursday
Alice—Friday
Paul—Saturday

13. Hotel Rooms

Malloy—6th floor
Brown—8th floor
Carley—16th floor
Wright—17th floor
Snow—25th floor

14. Beach Party

Jeff—red sandals—green towel
Ted—green running shoes—blue towel
Steve—brown loafers—brown towel
Chris—blue sneakers—red towel

15. Detective Dilemma

Detective Thrill—green book—well (solved the case)
Detective Zill—brown book—wall panel
Detective Pill—red book—safe
Detective Mill—blue book—cave

16. Collections

Robert—baseball cards and coins
Maureen—bugs and rocks
Joan—seashells and dolls
Bryan—stamps and comic books

17. Occupations

Kay—police officer
Jason—dress shop owner
Bill—teacher
Don—candy store owner

18. Talent Contest

1—Bill (tallest)
2—Maria
3—Frances
4—Abe
5—Perin
6—Abby
7—Ray
8—Josh
9—Kim
10—Ruth (shortest)

19. Pizza Party

Kent—cheese and anchovies
Tom—cheese and pepperoni
Fred—cheese, pepperoni, and sausage
Trina—The Works
Betty—cheese and bacon
Willie—plain cheese

20. More Houses, Boys, and Pets

Billy Brown—second house—green color—worm
Willie White—third house—blue color—bull
George Green—fourth house—white color—bear
Bobby Blue—first house—brown color—gorilla

Table Logic

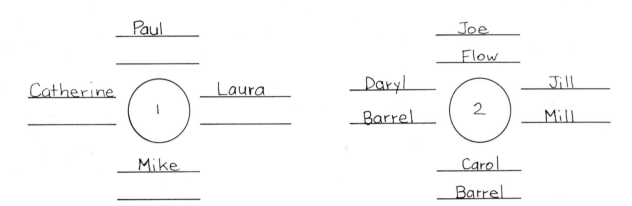

Table 1:
Paul
Catherine — 1 — Laura
Mike

Table 2:
Joe
Flow
Daryl — 2 — Jill
Barrel — Mill
Carol
Barrel

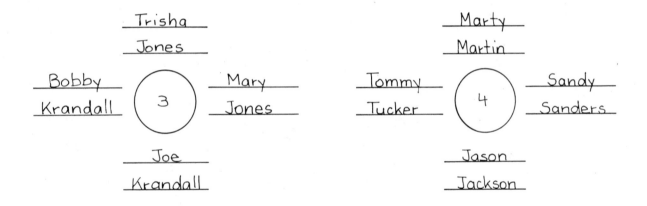

Table 3:
Trisha Jones
Bobby Krandall — 3 — Mary Jones
Joe Krandall

Table 4:
Marty Martin
Tommy Tucker — 4 — Sandy Sanders
Jason Jackson

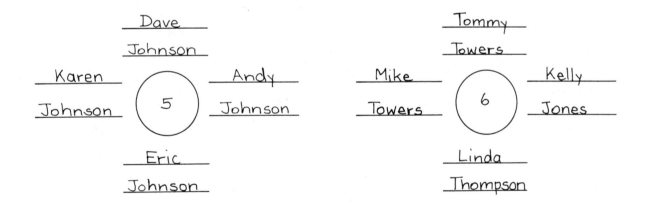

Table 5:
Dave Johnson
Karen Johnson — 5 — Andy Johnson
Eric Johnson

Table 6:
Tommy Towers
Mike Towers — 6 — Kelly Jones
Linda Thompson

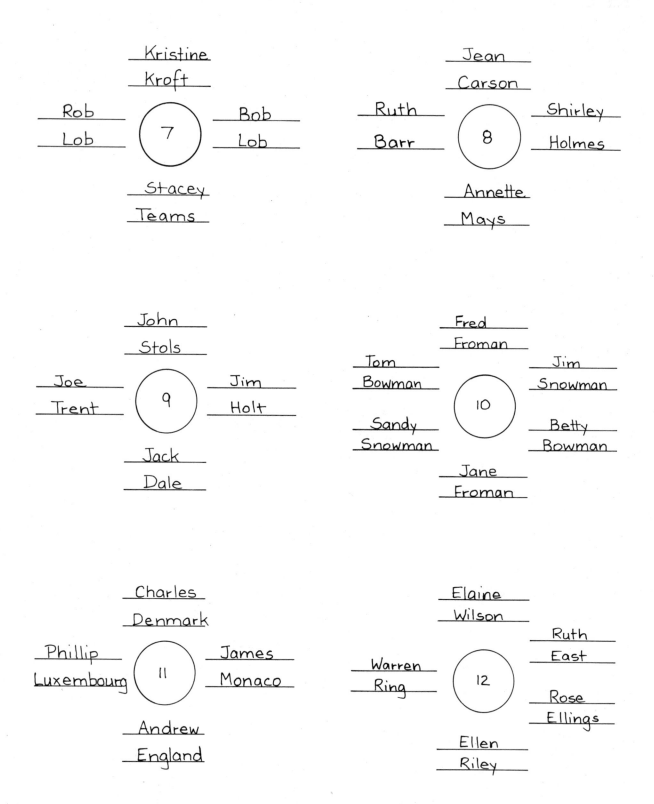

7
Kristine Kroft
Rob Lob
Bob Lob
Stacey Teams

8
Jean Carson
Ruth Barr
Shirley Holmes
Annette Mays

9
John Stols
Joe Trent
Jim Holt
Jack Dale

10
Fred Froman
Tom Bowman
Jim Snowman
Sandy Snowman
Betty Bowman
Jane Froman

11
Charles Denmark
Phillip Luxembourg
James Monaco
Andrew England

12
Elaine Wilson
Warren Ring
Ruth East
Rose Ellings
Ellen Riley

13

- Bev — I Love Lucy
- Kathy — news
- Joel — cartoons
- Earl — Little House on the Prairie
- Marty — sports specials
- Gordon — That's Incredible

14

- Sue
- Connie
- Rhonda
- Tim
- Bill
- Edna
- Kate

15

- John Johnson
- Karen Fillmore
- Jeff Beaver
- Lyn Adams
- Teri Moss
- Judi Johnson
- Paul Beaver
- Cindy Thompson
- De De King

Circle Logic

1. Drinks
1. Area 4
2. Area 5
3. Area 7
4. Area 6
5. Area 3

2. School Grades
1. Area 1
2. Area 3
3. Area 5
4. Area 2
5. Area 7

3. Reading Tastes
1. Area 4
2. Area 3
3. Area 5
4. Area 7

4. Cars
1. Area 1
2. Area 5
3. Area 3
4. Area 7

5. Summer Fun
1. Area 5
2. Area 2
3. Area 7
4. Area 1
5. Area 3

6. School Subjects
1. Area 3
2. Area 5
3. Area 6
4. Area 4
5. Tom would be nowhere

7. Are You Hungry?
1. Area 3
2. Area 4
3. Area 5.
4. Area 4
5. Area 6

8. Music, Music, Music
1. Area 5
2. Area 7
3. Area 3
4. Area 7

9. Gardens
1. Area 3
2. Area 6
3. Area 6
4. Area 1
5. Area 4
6. Area 1
7. Area 5
8. Area 2

10. Soft, White, and Furry
1. Area 5—a *white* bunny
2. Area 2
3. Area 3
4. Area 2
5. Nowhere
6. Area 2 if it's cooked; area 3 if it's not
7. Area 3
8. Area 6
9. Area 2
10. Area 4

Syllogisms

1. Valid
2. Invalid
3. Valid
4. Invalid
5. Invalid
6. Valid
7. Valid
8. Invalid
9. Invalid
10. Valid
11. Invalid
12. Valid

Syllogisms and Venn Diagrams

1. Valid
2. Valid
3. Invalid
4. Valid
5. Valid
6. Valid
7. Invalid
8. Invalid
9. Valid
10. Invalid
11. Valid
12. Valid
13. Valid
14. Invalid
15. Invalid
16. Invalid
17. Valid
18. Valid
19. Valid
20. Valid
21. Valid
22. Valid
23. Invalid
24. Valid
25. Invalid
26. Invalid
27. Valid
28. Valid
29. Invalid
30. Valid
31. Invalid
32. Invalid
33. Invalid
34. Valid
35. Valid
36. Invalid
37. Invalid
38. Invalid
39. Invalid
40. Invalid
41. Invalid
42. Invalid
43. Invalid
44. Valid
45. Invalid
46. Invalid
47. Valid
48. Invalid

Venn Diagrams

1.

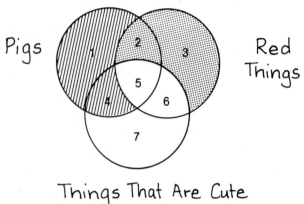

Valid

Look at the circles labeled *Pigs* and *Cute.* All of the *Pigs* circle that is outside of the *Things That Are Cute* circle (areas 1 and 2) is shaded in, or empty. The pigs are in area 5, which is within the circle of things that are cute. Therefore, all the pigs are cute. Disregard area 4 because it has been shaded in.

2.

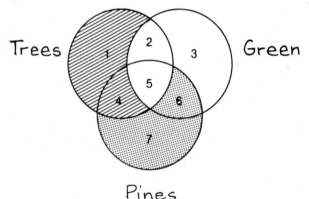

Valid

Look at the circles labeled *Pines* and *Green.* All of the *Pines* circle that is outside of the *Green* circle (areas 4 and 7) is shaded in, or empty. The pines are all in area 5. Therefore, all pines are green. Disregard area 6, because it, too, has been shaded in.

3.

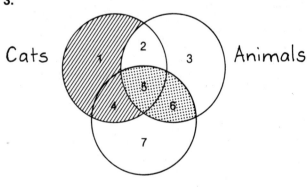

Valid

Areas 4 and 5 are shaded in, which means that they are empty. The shading means that there are *no* cats that are also plants. The cats are in area 2, which is outside the circle of plants.

4.

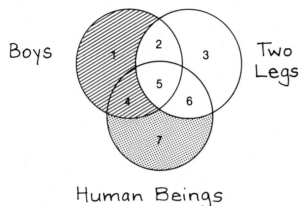

Invalid

To correctly diagram the conclusion, "all boys are human beings," all of areas 1 and 2 need to be shaded in. As you can see, the completed diagram does not show this. Area 2 has *not* been shaded in.

5.

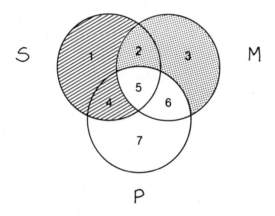

Valid

The areas of the *S* circle (areas 1 and 2) that are outside of the *P* circle have been shaded in. The *S* that remains is only in area 5. Area 5 is completely within the *P* circle. Therefore, all *S* is *P*.

6.

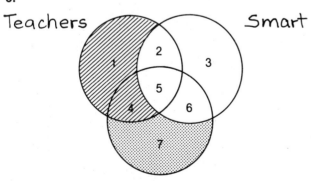

Invalid

Look at the circles labeled *Nice people* and *Teachers*. If all the nice people were teachers, areas 6 and 7 would be shaded in, or empty. However, area 6 has not been shaded in. Therefore, some nice people may not be teachers.

7.

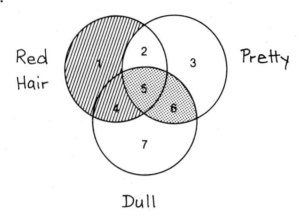

Valid

Areas 4 and 5 show where *Red hair* would be *Dull*. Those areas have been shaded in, meaning they are empty. Therefore, no red hair is dull.

8.

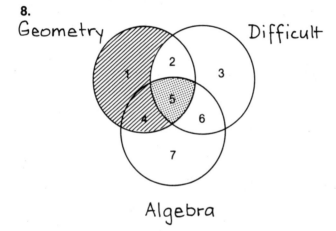

Invalid

Areas 5 and 6 show where *Algebra* is *Difficult.* If the problem were valid, both areas would be shaded in. However, area 6 has not been shaded in. Therefore, the problem is invalid.

9.

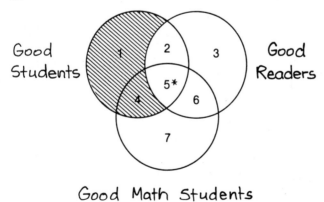

Valid

The asterisk, showing *some,* is in one of the areas (area 5) where the *Good math students* are *Good readers.*

10.

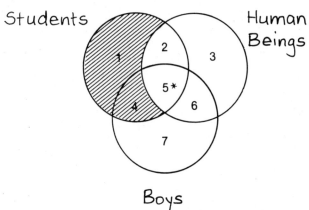

Valid

The asterisk, showing *some,* is in one of the areas where *Human beings* and *Boys* overlap.

11.

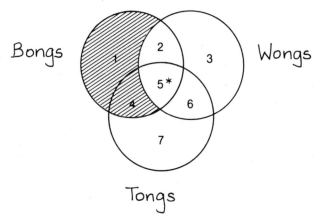

Valid

The asterisk, showing *some,* is in one of the areas (area 5) that shows that some Tongs are Wongs.

12.

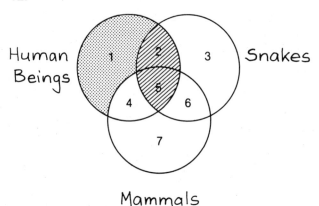

Invalid

Areas 5 and 6 show where *Snakes* are *Mammals.* Both areas would need to be shaded in (empty) if the syllogism were valid. However, only area 5 is shaded in.

13.

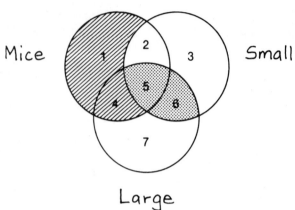

Valid

Areas 4 and 5 have been shaded in. This means that there are no *Mice* that are *Large*.

14.

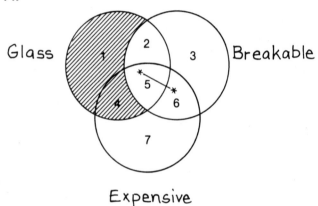

Invalid

From the second premise, you cannot be sure into which area you would place the asterisk. For the syllogism to be valid, the asterisk should be only in area 5. However, since the asterisk may also be in area 6, the syllogism is *invalid*.

15.

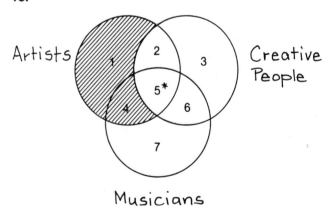

Valid

The asterisk, showing "some," is in area 5. This shows that there are some *Musicians* who are *Creative people*.

16.

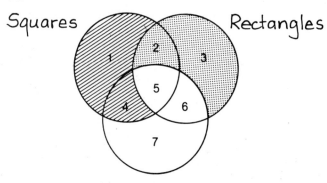

Squares

Rectangles

Quadrilateral

Valid

There are no *Squares* that are outside of the *Quadrilateral* circle. Areas 1 and 2 have been shaded in, thus showing that they are empty. The squares that remain are in area 5. Area 5 is completely within the *Quadrilateral* circle. Therefore, all squares are quadrilateral.

17.

Cars

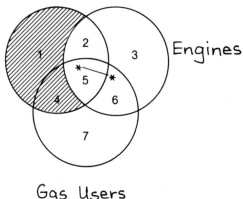

Engines

Gas Users

Invalid

From the second premise, you cannot be sure into which area you would place the asterisk. For the syllogism to be valid, the asterisk should be only in area 5. However, since the asterisk may be in area 6, the syllogism is *invalid*.

18.

Hamsters

Horns

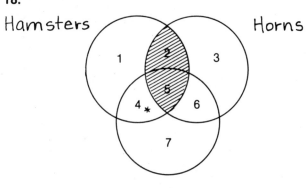

Furry Animals

Valid

The asterisk is outside of the *Horn* circle. This would show that there are *some* furry animals that *do not* have horns.

19.

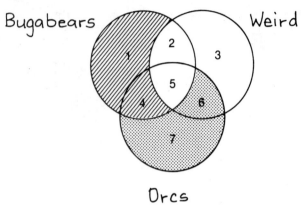

Bugabears Weird

Orcs

Invalid

To show the conclusion that all *weird things* are *Orcs*, all of areas 2 and 3 would need to be shaded in, or empty. However, they are not. Therefore, there may be *weird things* that are not *Orcs*.

20.

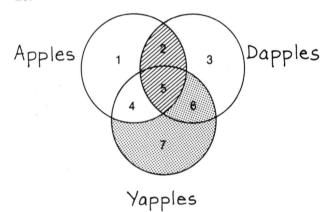

Apples Dapples

Yapples

Valid

Areas 5 and 6 show where *Dapples* are *Yapples*. Those areas have been shaded in; they are empty. Therefore, there are no *Dapples* that are *Yapples*.

ABOUT THE AUTHORS

Beverly Post and Sandra Eads are employed by the Torrance School District as teachers of mentally gifted youngsters. In addition to years of experience teaching in the gifted program, each author has taught at the regular elementary and intermediate level. Because of their varied backgrounds in the teaching field and their interest and experience in teaching logic to children, Post and Eads were selected by their school district to present a logic seminar for teachers at the annual California Association for the Gifted (CAG) Conference. They have presented many workshops on logic, while continuing to develop new and relevant materials for classroom use. They also assisted in the initiation and formulation of two school district publications, *WHODUNIT?* and *LOGIC LINKS,* which were developed for use by the grade school teacher.